In the Shade

FRIENDSHIP, LOSS, AND
THE BRUCE TRAIL

How lucky we are in Hamilton
to live so close to the
trails, forests & the strength
& solace they provide.

Marg Heidebrecht

 FriesenPress

Suite 300 - 990 Fort St
Victoria, BC, V8V 3K2
Canada

www.friesenpress.com

ISBN
978-1-5255-6015-6 (Hardcover)
978-1-5255-6016-3 (Paperback)
978-1-5255-6017-0 (eBook)

1. FAMILY & RELATIONSHIPS, DEATH, GRIEF, BEREAVEMENT

Distributed to the trade by The Ingram Book Company

For Megan and Morgan
and everyone who's ever walked with a friend.

"I meant to write about death,
only life came breaking in as usual."

Virginia Woolf

Introduction

There's an Excel spreadsheet on my laptop and a hard-cover journal on my bookshelf, both of which are records of the hikes Pam Will and I took to complete the 885-kilo-metre Bruce Trail between September 2011 and June 2015. The Bruce Trail Conservancy requests a detailed hiking log in exchange for an end-to-end number and badge; hence, the spreadsheet. The journal includes modest entries about the weather, the terrain, the shuttling to access the trails—so much about the shuttling, which can only be explained by the logistical challenge presented by that aspect of our adventure. Had I known that eighteen months after reaching Tobermory, Pam would reach under her arm and find a sarcoma, I would have written more, which, in turn, would have given me a resource when I decided to write these pieces. But we didn't know what we didn't know and set out on our journey unencumbered, unless you count the weight of multiple layers of clothing and an endless supply of snacks. This freed us, as my Headspace app reminds me, to be fully present, which is easier on trails, we discovered, than cross-legged on a hardwood floor. Our mothers never ventured off like this in their late fifties…not if there were crustless sandwiches to make or shut-ins to visit. Pam and I had been raised in that world but we attempted to model an alternative for our daughters; to balance work and home, self and others, and to lift our noses from the grindstone just a little.

Writing has given me focus and comfort since Pam's death in March 2018. Initially, I was offended when someone suggested writing was cathartic. I assumed they imagined the quality of the writing would be poor, intended for my tear-filled eyes alone, but if they meant I would wrestle with life, loss, and friendship in a way that has healed and enriched me, they were spot on.

When editing *III – Along,* a piece that describes the blazes that mark the trail's route, I cut the final paragraph, reluctant to reveal too much too soon. If you are a reader who takes the time to read the introduction, I know you are a reader who has already read the back cover and the acknowledgements, so this outcome will not be a surprise.

There's diversity on the journey of grief, and no common set of symbols can adequately address the spectrum of needs. I stumble on this ancient path, aware that countless others are staggering in adjacent lanes. The Bruce Trail taught me the perils of inattentiveness, the allure of ease, and the risk of distraction, all of which are relevant on the road I'm walking now and relevant, perhaps, to any who accompany me.

I - With

"So, what's next?" It's the question asked by each person steadying cake on an inadequate paper plate; a wedge sliced from a slab and decorated with one or more of the sugary letters contained in the phrase *Best Wishes on your Retirement.* It's not enough that the guest of honour has recently written reports, emptied a cubicle, and apologized to colleagues who now face additional tasks due to a hiring freeze. She hasn't yet enjoyed a Sunday dinner without restructuring it into Monday's packed lunch when she hears the predictable, and annoying, request for a meaning-filled timetable of what lies ahead. Not everyone mumbles or changes the subject. Pam's response is immediate. "I want to hike the Bruce Trail end to end," I overhear her say.

What? The Bruce Trail? That extraordinary, weather-beaten ribbon that guides hikers from Queenston to

Tobermory? Its slogan at the time is *Close to nature, close to home*. It couldn't be any closer to our homes. Five hundred metres from my side door. Tops. We walk every Thursday on trails that intersect and overlap its route as we count down the days of Pam's final semester. I know the guest list and menu for the celebration and have offered to make potato salad; how do I not know this? I too have contemplated more substantial walks on the Bruce Trail, but apparently never mentioned it to her. My goal is less ambitious; I envision a 134-kilometre walk home to Dundas from the trail's starting point, perhaps a re-set and reprieve after the mother-care, which at the time is consuming me, is done. The note I include in Pam's birthday card that August suggests we hike the section of the trail that skirts our community, then have lunch at a local café to discuss a bigger adventure. My treat.

Our conversation results in a plan that is as creative as it is cautious. Instead of setting out with map 1 in the *Reference Trail Guide*, proceeding until we conclude, or collapse, at map 42, we decide to start close to the nature that is closest to home. We'll follow the marked trail through the familiar Dundas Valley. Then, explore the gritty, urban route that zigzags up and down the escarpment in neighbouring Hamilton. Next, venture a bit to the south, a touch farther north on day trips with spouses, friends, drivers on local buses dropping us off, and providing encouragement. This modest initiation allows us to break in boots, augment picnic lunches, and buy poles for the steep sections and for the paths that become slippery on humid days or right after it rains. We consider twenty kilometres a sensible distance until the morning we labour on a stretch with a series of ascents-descents, relief coming only when the route crosses paved strips, all of which are named Mountain Road. Realizing twenty kilometres can cover significant differences in topography and conditions, we build flexibility, where possible, into the plan, take along the subsequent map, and choose an alternate finishing spot to recalibrate a bonus or penalty.

After ten walks on home turf, Pam advises we skip ahead to the Blue Mountain portion and tackle the logistics for the sixty percent of the trail that requires overnight accommodation, shuttling, and stamina. Maybe it is prompted by the years she worked as a camp counsellor, or summers spent hosting cottage guests, but I suspect Pam wants to establish our compatibility; a justifiable concern since three consecutive days on the trails requires us to be well-matched in essential ways not yet explored. In Collingwood, we confirm that we need thirty minutes to get from our beds to our breakfast, fewer if not assembling lunch from the contents of our cooler, and that we prefer to adjust the straps on our backpacks and be on our way, rather than sip a second coffee. The fifty-five kilometres we cover that weekend becomes the benchmark for multi-day hikes. No stops for photos or plaques describing the geology. Scenic lookouts only if it is time to drink water anyway and if there is a metre between us and a plunging descent. Snacks are crammed into pockets for constant access, but lunch is eaten when two-thirds of the hike is done. After dinner, we read books or flip through magazines, and shower but don't shop. Conversation is limited to reviewing the route for the following day, with more significant topics stockpiled to introduce and shore us up later on challenging terrain. We laugh at these consistencies and joke that there is no one else with whom we could tackle this adventure. The photographers, the dawdlers would find it restrictive and gruelling. The athletes, the tenacious? Chaotic and prolonged.

It helps our progress that we complement each other when it comes to the fear-worthy aspects of the trail. Pam dreads ladders, caves, and heights. Me? Cliffs, bears, and rattlesnakes. We set up a protocol. The confident one declares, "I'll go first," which leaves the other the opportunity to follow or refuse. Refusals require poring over the maps to back-track and modify the route. We agree to do this, but never have to. Not once. Crazy what camaraderie and a dash of peer pressure can do.

In spite of Pam's preference for structure and sequence, she proposes we leap ahead again to tackle a three-day piece of the Bruce Peninsula the following summer. It is reputed to be the toughest section, remote, with a variety of hazards; best to try it out while our resolve is high, and before our sixtieth birthdays. The July 2013 notes in my journal outline the difficulties encountered near Lion's Head—the day includes a misstep on slimy rocks with Pam landing hard on her tail bone. We have the habit of condensing the level of exertion to a pair of numbers; the first representing hard, the second, easy. Day one is summarized 90:10, underlined twice, the closest to quitting we ever come. We must have slept well because the next entry includes comments on the delicious breakfast and a reminder to buy an omelette pan when we get home. The synopsis of the other two hikes completed that week-end? 10:90.

With 454 kilometres accomplished over twenty-six days, we are halfway...not at the midpoint between Queenston and Tobermory, but in terms of total distance and number of hikes. Perhaps our approach is similar to the technique for jigsaw puzzles; find the corners and edge pieces, create a solid border, and then say "End to end" out loud.

Further similarities ease the second half of the journey. We have weekday flexibility and a tolerance for nasty weather; we pack lightly; we wear sunscreen, not make-up; we prefer B&Bs to campsites; we decline invitations from friends of friends who have an air mattress and live *sort of near* the trail. And, this is essential—we both like to talk. We already have a template for conversation that has evolved over three decades from our initial chats by the baby swings to a satisfying sequence that serves us well on eight-hour days. "How are the kids?" is first, never mind they are in their twenties and thirties, leading indepen-dent lives with careers and partners, and starting families of their own. We remember the names, places, and details of each other's extended families and give updates on situations described on previous hikes, confident that each understands the references of the other to a change in jobs, a pregnancy, or an illness. There is an invisible line, drawn carefully, cautiously, to mark where public ends and private begins, recognized by the phrase "having a hard time," followed by silence, or a pause. Pam is not inclined to gossip and I, who can be persuaded, once experienced a community implode—tongues twisting speculation into scandal, juicy titbits of lives tossed out like breadcrumbs for others to store or re-tweet. Never again. The line underscores both affection and respect for the people in our lives, but sometimes startles them. Pam checks with her daughter in the midst of a turmoil that is later resolved. "Can I tell Marg?"

The daughter smiles and nods. "I assumed you had."

Would our husbands be relieved or disappointed that we don't talk about them much? To some extent, that's because the four of us often have dinner in each other's homes and we hear their news first-hand. To a greater extent, it's because we, unlike hairdressers and therapists, don't press for details when "Driving me crazy" is muttered, as boots are placed on the path with an indignant thump. The bond between Pam and me deepens with each kilometre and if I knew the particulars of every disagreement with her spouse, I'd be in her corner, fuming long after they found their way through it. Those dinners in each other's homes? Awkward. A lesson, perhaps, for those who overshare, who don't consider an experience legitimate until it's posted on-line and several hundred friends have commented.

Next comes a discussion of books, movies, and eventually podcasts, the contemporary disruption to traditional radio, both of which enamour me. Pam is patient with my enthusiastic reviews of recent downloads even when I can't recall significant details like the last name of the program's host. She is less patient with recent technology as it tiptoes in, armed with distractions to resist and devices to recharge. She taught high school and knows what it can do to the adolescent brain.

During our busiest years, when work and family responsibilities limit our walks to ninety minutes once a week, this is the point in the conversation's arc where we use a frayed towel to wipe down a muddy dog, and say goodbye. Compare this to the Bruce Trail with its sweet, weightless air, the calming left-right tempo of our strides, and an abundance of time. Our habit of Pam walking ahead and me behind with no eye contact provides a comfortable connection...which parents driving teens to tournaments find out. Words, like our breath, are released from a deeper place. We now have time to talk about what's underneath. It's tempting to extend the alliteration of public and private with the addition of personal, but it's inaccurate. Personal implies identified, but not disclosed. I need a new word that captures the experience we have of pondering questions we've never asked each other or ourselves. "What held you back as a child?" "What worries you most on sleepless nights?" Perhaps a hyphen will do the trick. Self-discovery? Soul-searching? No, let's call this what it is. A gift.

There's a well-known quote about a tree, a forest, and a sound that no one hears. It's credited to the philosopher George Berkeley, who was theorizing immaterialism, unaware his words would be adapted into jokes that stereotype women and mock social media. Now I, too, revise the quote. *If a tree falls in my life and Pam's not there to listen, is the story complete?* My answer comes on a different day, on a walk with different people. A real tree, leafless and with a rotting trunk, roars its intention to collapse. I observe my quick-witted daughter enfold her young daughter and then drop to the ground into sludge that even the spiky, highest branches of the defeated tree can't reach.

Pam and I have established a pattern where we alternate between trees that are toppling over and arms that are breaking the fall. Most of the trees. For now.

I discover that a runner from Toronto starts his end-to-end on September 1, reaching Tobermory on the eleventh. We set out in September too, but our completion date is June 25, almost four years later. Apparently FKT stands for "fastest known time," but the acronym looks like "fuck it" to me. Our goal is unlike his. We maintain a moderate pace and an extended schedule to complete the trail injury-free and with our friendship intact. A surge in hours? An increase in back-to-back days? Our hip flexors and conversations would suffer. The compatibility we experience would decline into mutually, barely tolerant, identified by eye-rolling, arm-crossing, and prolonged periods of silence. FK that.

Our discussion topics are drawn from an ancient, diverse well. It is unlikely we could deplete it, but when I bump into Pam at the grocery store, I wave and then use my finger to draw a line across my closed mouth, zipping up and hoarding my news and queries for the next time we hike. Like the red squirrel who darts under my deck with walnuts, their value increases when stashed away for later consumption. The squirrel focuses her energy on gather, hide, repeat—she has instinct on her side. She knows that neither the first killing frost, which ushers in the dark, lean season, nor the appearance of snowdrops, that indicate its end, are hers to control.

Me? I've got a calendar on my iPhone that let's me schedule lunch for my 500th birthday in July 2454. I never consider we will run out of time. Not once.

II - Despite

"Have you always been an athlete?" It was a reasonable question given the setting; the locker room of a fitness club. I had bumped into a former neighbour when my daughter and I were on our way in and had mentioned I was preparing to hike the Bruce Trail. My daughter had looked after her kids, now grown, back when they needed someone to monitor DVDs and dole out Doritos. She was enjoying the late-day expanse of time that becomes available when parenting changes from constant supervision to exhausting weekend nightshifts; the adults ready for sleep, but the bedrooms of their offspring? Untidy and unoccupied. She was new to the gym, so I glanced over my shoulder to see which of the regulars, or perhaps instructors, she was talking to. The woman repeated the question, "Have you always been an athlete?" She was looking at me.

Athlete. A word reserved for those who hoist committee-approved bouquets above their heads and step up onto podiums; reserved for those who hold press conferences, who finger keys to resist texting while agents field questions about signing-bonuses and injury clauses; reserved for those tucked inside whirling, techno-fibre cocoons, waiting for the most advantageous moment to emerge, yellow-winged, and take off through the French countryside.

Had she asked me to hold a Massasauga rattlesnake, referred to in the trail guide book and always on my mind, while she tied a double-knot in her shoe laces, I would've been less startled. I don't remember how, or even if, I replied. I probably mumbled something inane and self-deprecating.

Like all unexpected questions that I'm incapable of answering with correct syntax, let alone integrity and coherence, this one's been hanging around, excessively persistent. Am I an athlete? When "Second Place is the First Loser" started appearing on T-shirts, the confidence of everyone without a championship ring took a major hit. Could the rest of us even whisper the word athlete, still use the emoji?

If I'm honest, the *we versus they* distinction came early, long before corporate America and Sportsnet developed business plans requiring fewer participants and more ticket-buying spectators. I was a little girl in an elementary school gym, who'd filled the summer with hopscotch, red rover, and countless varieties of tag. I had exclusive access to my best friend's two-wheeled bike—four-wheeled if you include the trainers, which were summarily detached—while she visited grandparents on the east coast. I swam on the shallow side of the bobbing buoy line in the local pool, then slung my duffel bag over my shoulder, plopped its matching sunhat onto my head, and skipped all the way home. I rested only to play jacks in the shade and called it quits when the street lights came on. Activity was my default setting. But in the gymnasium, I was baffled when each movement was timed, was measured for speed, for distance, and for accuracy. Clipboards were clutched, red ink was splattered. It felt like a betrayal rather than an evaluation. When the timepiece finally stopped clicking, I kept my eyes on my Ked sneakers and dragged myself back to the classroom. It had never occurred to me that school would include an assessment of my physical ability, and that this would trigger a confusing shift from bliss to brass tacks.

Tests in spelling, arithmetic, and even penmanship, were not a surprise. My older sisters had grumbled and boasted about their results, and I'd observed both the pattern and the high-set bar. New words (numbers, letters...) on Mondays. More practise on Tuesdays. Homework on Wednesdays. Thursdays, a dry run with sample questions as soon as the platter for Shake 'n Bake chicken and the empty Jell-O bowls were cleared off the kitchen table, and crumbs shaken off the embroidered cloth into the sink. All of this scaffolding was constructed before Fridays when the teacher handed out tests; damp papers with periwinkle-blue questions, students inhaling the unmistakable scent of the copy machine before unzipping their pencil cases. "No talking." "Keep your eyes on your own work." "Ten minutes left." "Pencils down." And finally, "See you Monday."

The progression was straightforward and predictable but not always successful, even in the time-honoured priorities of reading, writing, and arithmetic. It was effective for those who went to school every day, liked order, could sit still, grasped content the first go 'round, and had someone to quiz them on Thursday nights. It was a disaster for those who got sick, daydreamed, squirmed, required repetition, or got all three American networks on their TV, static free.

And then the pedagogical mystery. The familiar pattern was not used across the entire curriculum. Art, music, and phys. ed. instructors rejected it, perhaps under some illusion, or consultant's directive, that talent trumped teaching in these categories. The result? Some of us continue to draw houses with one door, five windows and a tree in the side yard. Even now, those relegated to the crow consortium only mouth the words while others sing "Happy Birthday" and the national anthem with gusto. And those, like me, who ran (but not fast enough), jumped (but not far enough), and (sometimes) caught the ball, became scorekeepers and referees. Those who could, did. Those who couldn't, sat on the sidelines and watched. Those who could got opportunities while those who couldn't got discouraged.

This tactic was successful when it came to painting murals in the foyer, to filling lead roles in *Oliver,* and to winning ribbons in city-wide track meets, but it was devastating for students who thrived in a context of colour, tunes, or movement in spite of modest observable output on their part. An entire system assumed that accomplishment was the measure of predisposition. And I swallowed it whole.

It took a while to reset the activity default position. Leaving high school was a significant nudge, as was turning thirty. Without shameful report cards disclosing marks in gymnastics and field-hockey, I was courageous enough to take up running, buy my own bike, and return to the aquatic centre. I know and have been told repeatedly that I am slow, but I don't care. When cyclists call out, "On your left!" prior to passing me, "Have a great ride!" is my breathless reply. When the early-bird swimmers want the worm that the fast and medium circuits represent, I dip my goggles in the ripples of the outside lane before slipping in with the other paddlers. Pam and I read blog posts about strenuous expeditions on the trail, then sit with maps to sketch out reasonable alternatives.

The importance of athletics to my accomplished and competitive high school peers has diminished. Some were injured in championship games and never fully recovered. Others were so conditioned by whistle starts and trophy finales that they are clueless in less-regimented contexts. Maybe this gives me an advantage—if you never win and are indifferent to losing, all that's left is playing the game.

The upshot is simple. I get grumpy when I haven't been on my bike for a few days. I don't hike because I have a dog; I have a dog so I can hike. And my favourite phrase in a theatre lobby is, "Ninety minutes, no intermission."

I very seldom bump into that neighbour, but suppose I did. Let's say at the deli counter. How awkward would it be for me, for her, for the clerk weighing shaved ham if my opening gambit were, "I now have an articulate response to that offhand question you lobbed my way seven...eight years ago." Awkward and unnecessary, because the person who needed to answer the question, to claim that predisposition to motion, endurance, and stamina was me. And yes, I've always been an athlete.

III - Along

Unlike Lao Tzu's journey that begins with one step, the Bruce Trail journey begins with one blaze—a single white blaze. The 885-kilometre span of the main trail is identified by white blazes, while the side trails use sapphire-blue to guide hikers through an additional 400 kilometres. The blazes are painted on trees, fences, rocks...whatever is available. A single blaze means go straight ahead. Two blazes let you know there's a turn. If the top blaze is a bit to the left of the bottom one, hikers veer left. A bit to the right? Veer right. I recently found out there are tuxedo blazes on the trail too. I'd been oblivious. Some resourceful person, realizing that white rectangles on light backgrounds were not always visible, devised a method of painting a black rectangle first, and then adding the white layer on top. Pam and I intend to follow these rustic tuxedos and their less formally-clad counterparts to complete the main trail. We occasionally need the blue blazes to lead us from shuttle drop-offs to less accessible sections of the main trail, but decide not to use them for further exploration. The primary path etched by the trail's founders is already 500 kilometres longer than the paved option taken by cars from Queenston to Tobermory. The proverbial crow trims another sixty-eight kilometres for a 310-kilometre flight. Show off. Eight hundred and eighty-five is plenty for us. It is reassuring to know that experienced hikers tramped here before us, used keen eyes to survey creeks, waterfalls, and rocky inclines. They experimented with routes through the most challenging spots until they plotted a course that did not require others to have the competence *or* confidence of coureurs de bois before lacing up their boots. I, for one, appreciate that.

With this straightforward marking system, how difficult can it be to stay on course and go, well, straight forward? Here's the paradox. It is easy when it looks hard, but hard when it looks easy. And here's why. We know we have to pay attention when scrambling up cliffs and wading across stream beds. We have to concentrate to find the blazes when our vision is compromised by dazzling sun or its less welcome opposite, torrential rain. Me: "There's one." Her: "Another one." Me: "Got it." Her: "This way." When the direction appears to be obvious, it is hardest of all. A wide, well-worn track intended for skidoos deceives us. Shared roads through provincial parks and conservation areas might overlap with us for a while, but at some point, we part ways. Unlike the poem, we forget to take the road less travelled and end up at random picnic spots or popular swimming holes before realizing we are literally off-track. The guide book has advice—evidently, we are not the only ones to slip up this way. Turn around and retrace your steps until you find a marker. Accommodating volunteers regularly repaint the symbols going both south to north and the other way 'round so we quickly, or eventually, glimpse a beloved blaze and the intended journey resumes. Crossing fields is another challenge. There are multiple times when we have to look across them, above crops and livestock, to locate a solitary tree towards which we are instructed to walk...walk like lemmings to the sea but compromised by tall grass, leafless branches, and grimy bifocals. Other missteps are of our own making. We are completely engrossed in conversation when one of us pauses, not to breathe, but to ask, "Seen a marker recently?" I wish I could say we are engaged in an analysis of Canada Reads manuscripts, or the voting record of our riding's incumbent politicians at all three levels of government. It's just as likely we are trying to decide how far above our crepe-y knees the hems of skirts should sit, or are swapping recipes for easy holiday meals that aren't simply complicated holiday meals with the prep done in chunks over several days.

Three kinds of errors; inattentiveness on easy sections, the allure of wide, welcoming paths, and our propensity to let discussion distract us. Most of our blunders fit one, perhaps two of the categories, but the mother of all mistakes, the mistake that prompts these mothers to revise the Nevada slogan to *What happens on the Trail, stays on the Trail* includes all three. We are delighted to find a B&B

that is situated *on*, not close to, or within driving distance of, but actually *on* the Bruce Trail. We have the mud of thirty previous hikes on our boots, and Pam pores over her notes and maps to see how the upcoming sections connect with the B&B's location. BINGO! The host will drive us to an access point twenty kilometres south of his property and we will walk directly back. No need to rise early, take two cars, park ours, and climb into his, which is the pattern on other mornings when the trail is close to, or within driving distance of our overnight accommodation. What could go wrong? We are confident and even though we take an after-dinner stroll through the large garden behind the house, never once consider checking to see where the trail crosses the extensive yard, its flowers and grass thriving in the ideal balance of sun and rain August provides that year. Cheeky. Most of the day is uneventful, and we have no need to consult the maps we tuck inside plastic sleeves to wear on lanyards around our necks. We do, to our credit, heed the guidebook's warning about logging roads and respect the detour put in place to avoid chairlift repairs at the local ski club. Mid-afternoon on the easy section with its wide, welcoming path cleared through tall wildflowers and lush grass, diverted by dialogue, we cross a country road that we assume is still south of our destination. Ten minutes. Twenty minutes. At thirty minutes, "Seen a marker recently?" It takes longer to switch from sunglasses to reading glasses than to pinpoint our error on the map. The trail crosses the same country road twice; once prior to and once past the B&B. The wide, welcoming path is actually part of the home's deep backyard but is, in our defence, not visible from the house itself. We walked (yes, talked) and overshot the correct turn. We stand on the shoulder of the country road, laughing at ourselves and this preventable predicament. The chuckles become chortles and the giggles grow into guffaws until eventually we wipe away the sunscreen and sweat that are stinging our eyes and start again. I wish a passing motorist had snapped a photo of us on that roadside; a memento of companions embracing not only the moment and each other, but the chaos too. Unencumbered, free from care.

The white rectangular blazes guide us to Tobermory, safe and sound. Too bad the rest of life doesn't have similar markers to show the way. I could've used that kind of clarity when deciding on majors, matrimony, kids, and careers. And I would welcome it now.

IV - Inside

The mother of my husband's late first wife (deceased, not tardy) visited us in the early 1980s after her own spouse died. Some might think it awkward but Edna, like me, married a widower who was already a father. If she had misgivings about my capacity to care for her grand-children, she kept them to herself. Over breakfast one morning, she recounted a dream from the previous night. I assumed it would be a nightmare depicting her daughter's decline and wondered how I'd answer questions posed by our curious toddler, sitting in her highchair playing with strips of peanut butter toast. I needn't have worried.

"It was a dream about threshers," Edna began. "Eight of them on our farm for three days, so I asked Aunt Rita to bake the pies, and what did she do? Baked one pie!" Eight men plus one pie equaled modest slivers, unless she used a deep-dish, ten-inch plate. Now I was the curious one. "How many did you need?" I asked.

"Well, for morning coffee alone we needed two, but there was afternoon coffee to think about, and some of the men liked my shoofly better than their own ma's so they snuck another piece after supper."

I did the math. A baker's dozen. Minimum. I reached into the box of Cheerios and placed a handful on my daughter's tray; something to occupy her so I could hear more. The men lived nearby and ate breakfast at home; oatmeal, a few eggs, toast, homemade preserves. In spite of the August heat, there was perked coffee with the pie at ten. Dinner was served at noon. A roast of some kind— beef, pork, chicken—served with whatever vegetables had survived the unpredictable pattern of sun, rain, and hail farmers had endured that year. More pie, more coffee and then supper; fresh bread, sweet butter, cold roasted meat and field tomatoes, sliced and stacked into heavy sandwiches, piled onto platters until huge hands scooped them up. Food was fuel, fuel for fourteen-hour days that began in the field where sheaves of wheat were gathered, and ended only when kernels were separated from the straw. Piling, pitching, lifting, carrying, and heaving. I doubt that today's fitness trackers, in spite of their complex calculations, can evaluate those activities. The required exertion leaves *moderate* intensity in the dust and even *vigorous* is inadequate since it's often misappropriated by those who sprint for an Uber. Thirty-five years earlier, the responsibility for feeding threshers was on Edna's, well, on her plate—thirty-five years of a persistent nightmare that there wouldn't be enough food, enough fuel for the team to complete their arduous task, a failure that, in essence, meant no straw to feed livestock over the winter, and no grain to sell. Devastating consequences.

Growing up in the city, I rarely thought of food as fuel. Sure, my father walked to his place of employment, seven minutes on his own, closer to ten when my sisters or I tagged along. He walked to the bank, to the post office, to the drug store and, once a week, climbed up half a dozen steps to preach from a pulpit. *Moderate*. My mother hauled a Hoover up to the attic, then down to the basement, lugged wet laundry out to the line, and wrestled with a floor polisher that had a mind of its own. Perhaps she embodied *vigorous*. Most food was prepared from scratch, though we just called it cooking. The disruption to consumption and nutrition, the shift from home-made to convenient, was looming and evident on grocery store shelves. Fat, sugar, and salt were injected into packages that promised tasty meals in minutes. Weary homemakers, my mother included, fell for the advertising. They dumped pieces of chicken and envelopes of chemicals into plastic bags, and gave them a shake. Hardware stores ran out of the Bundt pans required for a popular dessert made by whisking pudding powder into a cake mix, by adding some oil and a couple of eggs. Easy peasy. When it was time to clean up at my house, one sister washed while the other two dried, using hand-embroidered tea towels. The towels depicted kittens who were also drying dishes; doppelgangers stitched in poly-cotton thread. The kittens were grinning— omens of the grins and smirks, of Big Agra yet to come.

Hiking the Bruce Trail requires fuel. For the first time in our lives, Pam and I count to make sure we have enough calories; an unfamiliar, hefty tally after years spent reining them in to lose post-holiday pounds or atone for an extra glass of wine. Our food needs to be non-perishable, portable, and easy to prepare and digest. We experiment on the days we hike close to home. Bagels? Too dry. Mayo? Too dodgy. Stone fruit? Too easily bruised. By the time we fill the cooler for expeditions from base camp B&Bs, our menu is established and does not vary for the remainder of our fifty-two hikes. Each morning whole wheat tortillas are slathered with peanut butter, a banana set near the edge before rolling them into tin foil swaddles. Raw veggies, apples, grapes. We each bring our favourites, plus the ones that might wither in the crisper during our absence. Both of us pack trail mix, mine upgraded with Smarties and chocolate chips squirreled away and then salvaged from the right-hand drawer of my dining room hutch. Pam's oatmeal cookies nestle in her zipped lunch bag; I tuck mine into a front pocket, easily retrieved whenever I feel a little eleven o'clock-ish, which is early and often. Ample breakfasts are provided by our overnight hosts. Our choices are identical, apart from the glass of orange juice beside Pam's plate and the strips of bacon on mine. Multi-grain toast, eggs, fruit, yoghurt. We are fussy when it comes to baskets of baked goods. Scones fresh from the oven? Devoured, though muffins removed from six-cavity hinged containers are snubbed. Dinners are eaten at whatever local restaurant is within walking distance or a short drive away. There are numerous options when the Bruce Trail parallels ski hills. Forward-thinking developers lengthen and enhance the tourist season and now promote wineries, apple orchards, caves, and wall climbing. We take liberties with nutritionists' 80 (healthy): 20 (fat, sugar, salt) food rule, achieving a more stable and realistic 50:50. The first night we order burgers and fries. The following evening, salad, dressing on the side, and some kind of protein. Serving sizes are unpredictable and influenced by area code rather than price. In rural communities, beef-tallowed fries and garden-fresh produce spill off plates. Meat and fish are grilled, but moist. In cafes frequented by day-trippers from the GTA, freezer-burned patties rest on supermarket buns. Almonds and raisins are scattered on top of spring mix, with undercooked nuggets or dry skewers placed alongside. Meagre portions. Were we in our own kitchens, a bedtime bowl of cereal would be needed to fill us up. Weekday evenings, spring/late fall in remote areas, it is tricky to find a meal let alone a flight of beer. Early June mid-Peninsula is the worst. Had the B&B owner not been friends with the local chef, we might have unwrapped every Werther's caramel in the cut-glass bowl, chewed the limp celery left over from lunch, and called it a day.

Upon returning home, it is not uncommon to leave something behind in the other's car or backpack— whoever drives gives the passenger an extra set of keys and, early on, we realize it is convenient to keep our water bottles in the side pocket of the other person's backpack.

But when we hug goodbye, the keys and bottles, and sometimes wallets, boots, and travel mugs, are forgotten until the item is needed, prompting a phone call to arrange its return. "Are you starving today? Did you have breakfast and then, a half hour later, find yourself opening the fridge?" Yes, yes, yes. It makes me think about those threshers, and that dream. Did they, after weeks of sweating from farm to farm, spend the autumn months recovering, refueling? And Edna? I expect she removed the leaf from the Formica table, set down enough plates for her children, her husband, herself, and exhaled.

V– Underneath

"No bad weather, just bad clothing." I first heard the phrase when seated in the breakfast room of an Irish B&B. Steaming oatmeal, dense soda bread, chunky marmalade, Barry's Tea set out and intended to fortify our group of cyclists, provide us with fuel for a day of pedalling through a forest and past fields of sheep before grinding up and gliding down the coast of the sea. Outside the window, the mist gathered collaborators, morphing at first into light rain but ultimately into the current downpour—another slice of bread, an additional cup of tea as we put off our unavoidable departure with its equally certain outcome of slippery roads and soggy maps. No bad weather, just bad clothing. Saturated socks were not inevitable? I was a reluctant proselyte and modified my outdoor wardrobe gradually, but with each fully taped seam and breathable laminate finish, I became dryer and more zealous. With every Gore-Tex layer and Velcro ankle closure, I was warmer and soon preached to others with a fervour on par with those who chant, "It's Friday!" and wait for "But Sunday's a-coming!" in reply.

This conversion has served, still serves me well, both on and off my bike. As a cycling commuter, my personal best is minus seven degrees. I take my dog for hour-long hikes on days when others lead their canine companions to the closest patch of grass; they head for home with a disappointed dog and a disappointing umbrella—all of them wet. When it comes time to hike the Bruce Trail with Pam, I am good to go. Pam, as with most athletic undertakings and on the trail path itself, is several steps ahead. As a skier, longer, more comfortable days on the slopes motivate her, but it is most likely her upbringing in Sudbury and her mother's directive to dress in layers, wear mittens instead of gloves, and pull her scarf over her nose that underpins this expertise. We have clothing the proverbial letter carrier might don in snow, heat, rain, sleet, gloom of night, and we—okay, I—frequently and foolishly take all of it along, cramming inessentials into backpacks. Weighed down like Sherpas who accompany tourists to base camp.

We take our first hike the September after Pam retires when I still have a part-time teaching position in Hamilton at a college campus set close to the mountain brow. Looking north from my desk to the edge of the escarpment, the trail is less than a kilometre away; a bold, street-wise version of the footpath that, up to this point in the Iroquoia Section, has skirted the suburbs. Serene.

Here there is concrete, graffiti, trash. The trail perseveres under multi-lane mountain access roads, persists through the remains of an incline railway, and proceeds up steel-toothed stairs with step-training athletes. Mid-morning, mid-semester a colleague asks, "Is it safe?" I am nuking my coffee in the lunchroom and have just described the previous week's hike.

Her question startles me. Safe? What kind of safe? Personally safe in the way women take the hour, the light, and the crowd into consideration before heading out? Does she have concerns about the construction and configuration of the trail itself; is it steep, stony, unstable? Or has she too heard tales of wild things; not quite lions, tigers, and bears but rattlesnakes and bears which, I confess, also trouble me.

"Everything," she says. "Is it safe?"

My reply is quick and cavalier. "Oh, YES," but it gets me thinking. Up to that point our hikes have been repeats of well-known routes that weave through the Dundas Valley. We've tramped them numerous times with toddlers and teen-agers but now, in pursuit of our end-to-end objective and a badge, we are retracing some steps and logging the details. Concern for personal safety in my own backyard? Nope. I save that for far away, metropolitan areas where my anxious mind, unfairly, twists unfamiliar into unsafe. Plus, according to our timetable, the Peninsula Section is far away; it will take months to reach this 166-kilometre stretch with its spectacular views of Georgian Bay...and its rattlesnakes, and its bears. But there are twenty-seven guidebook maps between us and them. I will cross that bridge when I flip that page. The second kind of safe, the construction and configuration of the trail itself, remains. Do I trust the surface and slope beneath my boots? I am untested, bold, breaking in new Lowa Renegades when I answer, "Yes." If she asked me today, my answer would be a variation on no bad weather, just bad clothing. My answer would be, "No bad trails, just bad weather."

The *Bruce Trail Reference* offers a caveat in its introductory chapters advising hikers that conditions will vary according to the seasons and the weather, but like Ikea shoppers and iPhone users, most of us scoot through fine print to locate diagrams, details, and in this case, maps. Even the conscientious ones, who read the guidebook before filling baggies with mixed nuts and M&Ms, may assume it's bad weather that requires attention. The trails do indeed change, even mutate, so a less clear-cut answer is required for a second recurring question; "Is it hard?" Cautious peers considering a similar *Close to nature, Close to home* adventure, want to know. Pam and I exchange glances, shrug. "Depends on the weather."

The condition of the trail is impacted by the conditions of the atmosphere; temperature, wind, clouds, precipitation. The track beneath our feet can be dry, firm, wet, slippery, muddy, or icy and our view of it clear or obscure. Some twenty-kilometer days tick all the boxes. We cross bridges, stiles, and boardwalks built from wood, and yet again find they can be dry, muddy, or slippery. Mother Nature scores one—municipalities zero in terms of post-storm recovery; puddles remain on the shoulders of side roads long after rain in the forest is absorbed back into the ground, water trickling into creeks by the time we remove our hooded ponchos and find our sunglasses. We position our boots on bare earth, exposed rock, spongy moss, gnarled roots, dusty gravel, gummy asphalt, damp grass, and layers of leaves. The upshot is my gaze settles somewhere between Pam's heels and my toes; a position resembling the twenty-first century distortion of posture dubbed the "cell-phone slouch." In my defence, I have no choice. This is not a walk in the park. Steps are required before taking steps. Scan and scrutinize the path for twigs that could be roots, leaves that cover ruts, surfaces with mud or moisture, which like banana peels result in a struggle to regain balance, hilarious only in parades when it's the padded bottom of a clown that hits the ground with a thump. Plan the next footfall and hope you remember the plan before your foot falls or *you'll* fall since your eyes are now focused farther ahead. Repeat for 885 kilometers.

The guidebook is designed to concentrate on, "Is it going to be hard today?" On the back of each map is a written explanation that includes keywords such as *rugged, steep, crevice, alert, extreme caution* plus reassurances of *well-defined, grassy field, farm track* in paragraphs that describe the route from south to north. However, Pam and I piece together a non-linear journey that takes shuttling, accommodation, and distance (from home and on the track) into account. As a result, we travel north to south twenty-five percent of the time. On those days we are aided by blazes that mark the route in both directions, but the trail descriptions become linguistic puzzles. We read from the bottom of the page to the top, converting *ascent* to *descent, enter* to *exit*. The angle of *steep* remains constant but pain in our knees reminds us to translate *climb up* to *inch down* slopes.

In addition to these published warnings and reassurances, we are counseled by other hikers. Most give well-balanced advice, though the candour of a few throws us for a loop. On one occasion, Pam runs into an acquaintance who uses the word treacherous—*treacherous,* to describe a short section that is a stone's throw from the library in which they are checking out books. She is breathless when she calls me and both of us scratch our heads since we've been on that trail multiple times. Treacherous? Not that we recall. We were several decades younger, and possibly distracted by doling out graham crackers to the children who accompanied us.

When the day comes to tackle it, we brace ourselves. My husband drops us off early to give us extra time to navigate the horror that looms ahead. One kilometre. Nothing. Two kilometres. Zilch. Confused yet relieved, we pause for water before entering the tunnel that leads us under a well-travelled highway to tranquil woods and an old homestead. One of us, probably me, is smug. "We've gotten good at this." Skilled, adept.

The other, probably Pam, shakes her head. "It's dry today. A hint of frost, some wet leaves, and that climb, and those stairs would be slick. Very slick."

I remain unconvinced. "But treacherous?"

She nods. "Uh huh."

I hang onto my doubts for two and a half years until, on the outskirts of Wiarton, the tables are turned. It is October and we are near the end of a fifteen-kilometre day, the conclusion of the Sydenham section, which is muddy but manageable until we reach the route down the escarpment. The ingenious method of descent includes a double ladder and stone stairs. To this day my heart races when I remember hesitating, then taking off my backpack and tossing it across a gap in the rocks before descending. Manageable becomes difficult. Below us, someone is building a deck, the sound of a drill competing with the golden-oldies on a radio. Am I going to tumble down while Ben E. King sings "Stand by Me"? Seriously? Not so skilled and adept after all. We survive, stop in town for coffee before driving home, and chat with a couple at the next table. "Been hiking?" Our grubby appearance gives us away.

"Yeah, four amazing days!"

Silence, and then, "What did you think of those ladders?"

We reply instantly, in unison. "Treacherous."

The specifics of our expedition are gradually transferred from scrap paper to columns on a spreadsheet. Unlike other hikers who snap, post, and share, there are only three photographs from our entire trip with its convoluted route. On the morning of our thirteenth hike, we pose for our first photo at the southern terminus in Queenston Heights Park under the gaze, perhaps frown, of General Brock. The second photo captures celebratory grins at the northern terminus in Tobermory several years later. It is taken, truth be told, two days *before* we complete our last and final piece. We hike backwards, in the rain, through *extremely rugged* and *remote* to arrive at marker 127.5, map-41, the unpretentious Crane Lake Road.

Google recently reached into the chaos of my computer and recovered the third photo, an awkward selfie from that day. Unaware of YouTube's recommendations to hold the camera to the side, look up, and spin to find the light, we appear pensive rather than pleased. In our round-about way, we reach our destination, but our extraordinary adventure is over. This hike is the last hike. We change into running shoes, deposit our grimy boots on a threadbare towel in the back seat, and steer the car toward home.

There will be more walks together in the two years that follow; some in the Dundas Valley, a few at the mall, their length and pace decreasing with Pam's energy. There are no photos of our final walk together. It is short, unhurried, and takes us from her living room recliner down the hallway to her bed. She guides her walker, slides her slipper-clad feet along the hardwood floor and I, as always, follow a few steps behind. Stormy weather indeed, and nothing to protect us from it.

VI - Amidst

My aunt was not alone when she walked to the front of the church to whisper goodbye to her husband, a handsome and dignified man who reminded me of a Hollywood actor whose name I can never recall. A preschooler hopped beside her, too young to recognize the solemnity of the occasion and too enthralled by her tippy-tappy shoes to travel up the aisle sedately; a great-grandchild who had probably been told there would be cake later, but was reminded to stay quiet and sit still for now. And as the grieving widow clutched the hand of the child, I expect the same thought-bubble floated above the heads of each person shifting to find a comfortable position on the wooden pews. *Ah, the circle of life.*

There is truth, and modest comfort, in the thought that the decline and death of some is balanced by the arrival and activity of others; family trees lose decaying limbs even while buds are forming. The candor of little ones releases cool and welcome air into stuffy reception halls, like the time my three-year-old cousin, observing the post-funeral arrival of buckets of crispy fried chicken, commented, "Grandpa's missing the best part!" Grandpa, of course, was dead.

The circle of life remains a philosophic construct, one of the clichés that, along with "Only the good die young" and "Time heals" is tossed from one mourner to another in a culture that prefers distraction to eye contact until Pam gets sick, really sick. The beginning and end of life line up, collide, and overlap, which causes me to take hold of that circle and wrestle it into a new shape. Pam comes home from the cottage and calls me before coming over for dinner on our deck. "I shaved my head," she says. "Didn't want the scarf to be a surprise." Hats, scarves, wigs replace the chin-length bob that was long enough to pull back into a pony-tail and tuck into the gap at the back of her baseball cap should yard work or lakefront duties require it. "How's everything?" she asks, referring to my daughter and daughter-in-law, both of whom are pregnant, due that autumn just weeks away and weeks apart. Even as I fill her in on recent ultrasounds and appointments with midwives, I'm aware that I'm squeezing that legendary circle inside my fist—hard and, like a balloon, the ends expand and almost burst leaving me with what? An oval? An ellipse? A dilemma?

Invitations into the lives and bedrooms of the newly born and soon to die can't be presumed or coerced, so when I'm welcome in the homes of my infant grandsons and my weakening friend, it's a privilege that I fear might become a predicament. I'm less anxious about organizing my schedule than I am about coping with disparate emotions. The events in each home are unique, but they hold in common the constant requirement that I be present—entirely present. Some of the presence is easy and some more difficult. It's not simple or predictable. Time with the babies includes both cuddles and chaos, and time with Pam, both connection and catastrophe; staying present prevents my mind from weaving endless "what ifs" into a coarse, knotted tent of despair. The circle of life isn't an ordered cycle like the one that depicts egg, caterpillar, chrysalis, and butterfly on colourful posters in science classrooms. My ellipse contains loving energy that moves like waves from early life to later life and travels back again with warm, soothing water that trickles over and around us. Think water balloon meets Slinky.

The weeks take on a rhythm that includes different days in different households, leaving my husband to walk the dog, to shuttle me to GO stations, and to provide meals and moral support on my return. One of the grandsons is the second child and his father, my good-natured son-in-law, welcomes my visits since it means an uninterrupted sleep in another room. On these night shifts, I wrap sweet Arlo, burrito-style, before settling him in the cradle on a mattress with a bit of an incline. Tummy trouble. When he wakes, I carry him in to my daughter and sit beside her in the dark. She nurses him before passing him to me to coax out a burp. Sometimes we are quiet, too tired to talk. Sometimes, when our days together are filled by the antics of and attention to their toddler, the middle of the night is when she asks about Pam. I tell her of the unsuccessful drug trial and the trips to the ER, all while breathing in the milky breath of the little one whose mother, decades earlier, I nursed and re-settled, albeit on her side and under a crocheted blanket, hoping against hope that she would sleep.

Closer to home, I ride my bike to my son's house and enter on tiptoe in case baby or new mom or, fingers crossed, both have been able to sleep. I've paid attention to the layout of their home and can fold laundry, blitz the kitchen, and provide a simple meal without asking my exhausted daughter-in-law too many questions. I know how to do this—need, in fact, to do this. It's a bonus when summer weather makes a brief comeback and I can sit in their yard, drape a muslin throw around precious Elliott, and kiss his neck while he drifts off to sleep. My mornings with Pam take account of sleep too, though unlike the babies for whom the time between naps lengthens, Pam's days include additional, sustained periods of rest; initially on the sofa, then on the reclining chair, and ultimately on the hospital bed brought in to accommodate her limitations and discomfort. In spite of being content to talk, or not talk, and thankful to be sitting beside her, sadness overwhelms me. It leaves me gasping as if a bully were shoving boney elbows into the decades of our tender companionship. I inhale in an attempt to calm myself and hope my brain remembers the article I read on-line and releases the right hormones. When I exhale, fully and through my mouth, as mandated, I feel a bit better. Pam dozes peacefully beside me. Could it be I've breathed in her strength?

The expected tension in my back and tightness in my jaw seldom materialize. It's as if my time with the infants melds together with my time with Pam, and creates a fortifying mixture like the ones flogged by itinerant hustlers during the Depression, or concocted by attentive Kanga for reluctant Roo. The image of baby, mother, grandmother, dying friend does *not* produce an attractive poster for any classroom, and yet it captures the essence of a deeper reality that exists when we enter the messy aspects of our passage on planet earth. It's an amplification of the original archetype; the circle of life on steroids. I know. I experienced it...am experiencing it still.

VII - Without

When my daughter, Christine, went to nursery school, we formed a carpool with three other families and their daughters, all of whom were a similar age. Katie, Julia and their families participated primarily because of geography. We lived within blocks of each other and the nursery school was too far to walk. The location of the third family's home was out of our way, but Christine and their daughter, Sophie, had already spent two of their three tender years going back and forth for weekly swaps and would continue this routine for after-school care, often with a younger sibling in tow. This gave Sophie's dad time to write his PhD thesis and me time to breathe. "Two peas in a pod," my mother-in-law commented, watching them fill hours with imaginative play. They sought each other out in the classroom too.

One morning, en route to Sophie's house, Katie sat in the back seat with Christine and Julia, munching on toast as the peanut butter and honey dripped over its edges, adding a new seam of archeological treasure to our '82 Phoenix. "When will you play with me?" she asked Christine. The question was straightforward and direct. I expect she had observed Christine and Sophie in their Montessori Casa, tracing metal insets (which I misunderstood as *insects* until the Spring Open House), pouring rice from one pitcher to another, and descending on the snack table together. Katie wasn't whining or grumbling. She seemed to be looking ahead at the week, perhaps a budding extrovert filling her academic dance card.

Christine was quiet for a minute and then replied, "Maybe when Sophie dies."

I don't think she intended to be hurtful, though a mother's not often the best judge of her child's intentions. My gaze shifted from the road to the rear-view mirror, optic nerves on fire until I caught a glimpse of Katie's face. Her chin maintained its andante tempo as she finished off the stubborn crust, but it did not quiver. I detected no distress pooling in or dripping from her hazel eyes. The question had been asked and answered, allowing the conversation to turn to the contents of the best treat bags ever. All three girls agreed on gummy worms and slap bracelets, but disputed the value of pencils because, as Julia contended, they were essentially school supplies. I explained the word "essentially" to the other two.

Maybe when Sophie dies. My daughter's connection to Sophie was so well-established that she could not envisage either the need or desire to play with anyone else. Unless, of course, Sophie was dead.

Friends do die. Pam is going to die. I happen to be in her kitchen one Monday when the palliative physician visits. A PSW is giving Pam, by then confined by the perimeter of a 39"X75" adjustable bed, a sponge bath. The doctor and I perch on stools drinking the coffee Pam's husband Al makes before excusing himself to take a call or reply to a text; one of the dozens that require him to be an administrative assistant and advocate, in spite of his anguish. We talk briefly about various hospice and palliative settings in the city. I'm familiar with the places and processes and tell him of my recent decade in the upside-down world of eldercare where adult children push the wheelchairs of the ones who pushed their prams. The physician listens, then puts down his cup and pauses before quietly posing this question. "Have you ever lost a close friend?"

Now it's my chin that quivers. I shake my head, "No."

Good reviews, and his unflinching query, prompt me to borrow a recently-published book on grief from the library. I read the acknowledgements, glance at the author's photo, and skim the table of contents. *Partner, child, parent.* Not a word about friends, which causes me to toss it onto the pile of books on my night table. Later that day I retrieve it and jot down the title knowing there are others in my circle for whom these particular losses resonate. And although I've been orphaned for a while, it's reckless to assume I'll never need the final chapter's tips for maintaining a routine in the wake of the other two devastations the author has embraced.

It *is* different when friends die. Maybe the author of the book was overwhelmed, unable to distinguish acquaintance from ally or colleague from companion to complete an honest fourth chapter with the speed and precision the editor required. Maybe the publishers didn't want to include friends in the first place. Were they young, untested? Had death tapped only the rim of their existence when it summoned elderly, enigmatic relatives who lived several provinces away?

Palliative teams consider *partner, child, parent* of their patients during the sacred hours that precede death. It's extraordinary that the head of this group expands his attention to include the patient's friend and takes a moment to attend to me. His words are simple and sad. "Brace yourself."

I'm sure that this doctor's CV is lengthy, that students invite him to connect on LinkedIn, but I doubt there is anything in his decade of post-secondary education or an on-line conversation window that motivates him this Monday morning in Pam's kitchen. I suspect he, like me, once sat with a close friend and placed tiny ice-cubes onto a dry tongue. Perhaps a kind person offered him the wisdom he now extends to me, though it's also possible no one did, which would explain his vigilance, his desire to prevent anyone else from underestimating this loss. Regret may lie beneath his steady demeanor like tectonic plates beneath the earth's crust, unnoticed until they shift and crash into each other, causing tidal waves that leave him gasping for air, and eruptions that conceal the sun behind a fragmented haze.

When it's time to leave for home, I say, "I love you," to Pam, and then, "Good-bye." There are a handful of visits yet to come and they end the same way, with the same words. I have been warned.

VIII - Between

A few years ago, over lunch, how fitting, someone introduced me to the concept of conversation pies. It's been a helpful image that explains why certain social events, particularly shared meals, are successful and others disappointing. Available airtime, like a pie, is divided among the number present. Five people? Each should be allotted one-fifth of not only the Dutch apple or lemon meringue, but also the conversation pie. During the event, each person talks one-fifth of the time. Ideally, everyone else listens during their remaining four-fifths, but whether they simply plan a rebuttal, daydream or, in this day and age, check their phones, is up to them. There are challenges. No one knows, upon arrival, how long everyone will stay, making it impossible to calculate total minutes and create equal portions. Without a sophisticated stopwatch, how can turns be tracked? Besides, discourse is fluid, words overlap—people have more to say about some topics than others. An additional snag is the introvert-extrovert mix. The reserved guests, reluctant to interrupt, wait for miniscule pauses so they can join in. Confident folks are unaware and help themselves to seconds of, well, the seconds. But when it does work, departing guests linger at the door with offers of, "Next time, my place." Walking home, they rehash the food, the drinks, the music, the guest list, the themes of both the cheerful chitchat and the deep discussions, but can't quite pinpoint what made the evening exceptional. And the hosts, in spite of cleaning and cooking, feel exhilarated, not exhausted. They blow out candles, put away leftovers and agree not only to gather up glasses but also to scrub the pots, giving them another hour to savour the delicious, elusive outcome of their equitable pie.

Given this high praise, one might conclude that all conversations benefit from the application of the template. Not so. Consider anxiety, heartbreak, loss. Listeners in these situations need to hold out, not onto, airtime. They need to forgo the formula, pass over the precedent. Bite their tongues. However, once the dialogue dance has been committed to memory, it's hard to step back. We recognize the introductory lyrics, "How are you? What's up?" We sway back and forth and hum the melody. Oblivious.

Grief is the worst time for a conversation pie and yet it seems to be our default setting. One: "My ----- just died." Another: "Oh, I know what that's like. I had a ----- who died too." We mistake it for empathy. I know because I did it for years; gave details of illness, side effects of treatment. Pot, kettle, black. Desperate to tell our own stories, we cut the already-wounded off at the knees. We assume we are being helpful, but if we really remembered what it was like when our mother, or brother, or friend died, we would stay quiet. We would let the other person speak, or in unbearable silence, ask gentle questions; "What was she like?" Never "How old was she?" This implies there's a magic number below which death is (gasp) tragic and above which it's a (shrug) given. Offer the pie in its entirety; bronze crust, saccharine filling, and twisted lattice; the bits that bubble over and burn onto the plate's rim.

Now it is me who chokes on the words, "My friend just died." In those raw, early days of grief, two people, on different days and in contrasting situations, serve this mode of kindness up to me. The first is inside a grocery store, that chaotic space that's the entrance but also the exit. The area where unwieldy carts collide and baskets are stacked, awaiting those who need rotisserie chicken and a bag of mixed greens. I am going in; she is coming out. We were once in a carpool, ferried daughters to nursery school, daughters who now have families of their own as well as advanced degrees and meaning-filled employment. This woman is good-natured and well-read, but we never made the leap from meeting at the shared activities of our children to setting up additional times to get together. Never became close friends. At that time, we were the ones juggling families, advanced degrees, and meaning-filled employment. Still, we always chat when we bump into each other which, given that we live in the same town, is surprisingly seldom. "How are you?"

There are two answers to this question. "Fine. You?" And the honest one. Soothed by her warm smile and submerged in sorrow, I choose the latter. "My friend just died."

The smile dissolves. She sets down her groceries, freeing her hand to rest lightly on my arm. The death itself is not news. She recognized the photo in the paper. Has, in fact, cut it out, and used a magnet to put it on her fridge. No, her devastation is for me. She didn't know I am a close friend of this lovely woman, whose path of child-rearing with its swimming lessons and school council meetings has been similar to hers and has, on occasion, overlapped.

The automatic doors continue to slide, at times to ease the arrival and departure of shoppers, but our modest gestures, shrugs, and even sighs are also detected by the electronic eye that keeps one step ahead of the steps of customers. Open and close. People jostle past us. Not once does she check her bag to see if the ice-cream is melting. Not once does she reposition her left wrist to glance at her watch. I don't know how long we talk. Maybe ten minutes, possibly twenty. All I know is that I say my fill while she listens and nods, her face reflecting heartbreak back to me. I'm not sure my lament is even coherent. "It hurts, it hurts, it hurts," like a child who tumbles off roller skates or a bike and is waiting for mercurochrome and a Nurse Nancy Band-Aid. Every "Ooh, oh no," she proffers is salve, balm, cool astringent. I can't remember if she hugs me, but I know she encloses my grief. And her own losses? She sets them down.

The second pie is provided a few weeks later by a woman I met when our sons were in kindergarten, that carefree introduction to academia as it existed before morphing into full days and adding a junior partner. This woman is well acquainted with grief. The rug was pulled out from under her two years earlier. Her husband, who exercised, meditated, watched his diet, and played basketball, felt a little off one morning, slumped over in his chair a few hours later, and died. They had a solid marriage and had recently welcomed grandbabies and modified schedules to reduce responsibility and add adventure. His death was unexpected and bewildering to acquaintances and neighbours but devastating for those he loved. No warning, no good-byes. A deplorable departure.

We plan to walk dogs together one evening and agree to meet at a neighbourhood intersection dubbed the three-way stop. She, of all people, could expect half, if not more, of the pie. There's an implicit hierarchy in loss—child and partner at the top, with parents and siblings next—and, as a widow, she is clinging to the top of a ladder she never wanted to climb. "These things have helped me. Nature, children, grandchildren, dogs," she says. "And friends, of course. My friends have been amazing." Prudent counsel as she hoists my grief, all grief, up from the bottom rung of bereavement and places it alongside hers.

Our canine companions and forest trails console me, confirming the wisdom in her advice, but I talk a lot too. I don't recall how far we trek before I stop licking the pie plate and offer her the remaining crumbs to ask, "And you?"

It's courageous to speak of death at all in this culture where three days off plus a mixed bouquet equals done and dusted. We never know who will rescue us; who we, in return, will rescue. There's an elusive formula that considers decease date and closeness of connection to determine the course for conversations. Alternating slivers, whole pies. We often get it wrong. But when we settle into this unfamiliar landscape and clear space for the losses of others, we dignify our own loss and position death smackdab in the middle of life, the only place it has *ever* really occupied. Here, pragmatists are able to examine it and philosophers reflect on it while mourners, in its shadow, catch their breath.

IX - Beyond

A few months after Pam dies, I'm on a plane crossing the Atlantic. The configuration of the aircraft, and my husband's desire for an aisle seat, place me beside the window. Since new cost-saving measures limit in-flight entertainment and neither of the books I brought along are compelling, I watch as the final bags are loaded, then skim the card that outlines the protocol for various emergencies. Aeronautical engineers use extensive knowledge of lift, drag, thrust, and weight to design this winged means of transport, but when the airplane tips its nose, like a dog tempted by an unknown scent, and we lift up and off the runway, it feels more like magic than physics. Agitated passengers fumble with devices, waiting for clearance to turn them back on. Weary passengers adjust U-shape pillows and pull pashminas over their heads. I return to the view outside my window and catch a final glimpse of the structure and surface of the city, and its two million tiny inhabitants. Then, the clouds, as if a sweet-toothed alchemist, rejecting lead and gold, has turned to whipped cream and marshmallows and transformed them into this unending, untainted expanse of white. And, out of the blue, above the blue, I start looking for Pam. It startles me, but shouldn't, since my secular and spiritual roots support limbs on which persistent images are fastened; angels knocking down pins in a bowling lane that slices through clouds, St. Peter flipping through records on a lectern that rests on clouds, elaborate staircases that end at wrought-iron gates nestled among clouds. A theme. Will Pam be standing, sitting, awake, asleep? Before I can settle on her posture, the plane's ascent is complete and the pilots, or their digital associates, make the necessary adjustments to the higher, cruising altitude. Spotting her now is unlikely.

The dead—where are they? I'm not alone in my query. A multitude of philosophers and everyone who grieves asks this, plus the longer question that accompanies it. *What comes after what is supposed to be the end?* I'm an anxious apprentice awake in the night when I add this extension. *When do they actually leave?* ER physicians look at the clock before pronouncing *time of death*. Forensic pathologists at crime scenes aren't as precise, but their estimates are crucial to investigations that follow. Both groups would be exasperated by my disregard for their respective markers; cessation of breathing and heartbeat, rigor mortis, and body temperature. I'm embarrassed to admit using Wikipedia, but encouraged to read that bones, skin, and tendons endure twelve hours after the chart's filled in and next-of-kin notified. Maybe there is some wiggle room.

Decades earlier, a different death but the same question. I arrived at the hospital to visit Annie, a friend in decline. She was elderly, weary, and now very sick. I was one of several who had provided weekly transportation, manoeuvred her into my front seat, and wedged a stubborn wheelchair into the trunk of my car. Unaware she'd been moved, I proceeded to the ward where I'd seen her the previous week only to find someone unfamiliar in her corner of the four-person room. No one was available to redirect me, so I retraced my steps and approached Patient Information in the foyer. "Yes, a new room." The volunteer gave me the details. By the time I waited for the elevator, followed the signs and found this new room, my friend was dead; alone, except for the nurse who walked in ahead of me, and turned around to ask "Family?"

I shook my head.

"You have to leave." Harsh. She looked at the clock and made a note of 2:15. I should have told her that my friend's children lived miles away; one in another country. I should have told her I wanted to sit by the bed for a while, but I was young and the part of me that was intimidated by clipboards and uniforms and feared being sent to the principal's office, nudged me into the hall.

When did Annie actually leave her body, that bed, the building? Where was she when her breathing changed, sped up, slowed down, stopped, resumed? Was she outside, hovering above the hospital when I arrived, watching while I too sped up and slowed down through side streets looking for non-metered parking? Or was she inside floating through corridors, searching for me while I searched for her? I found a chair and sat in the hallway near her room, hoping she was still there. It had been years since her bones had held her upright—allowed her to walk unassisted. Maybe they needed the twelve supplementary hours I had read about to support her transition from this world to the next. I waited.

When my father was dying, he was not alone. My mother, like the adjustable meal tray and the hinged television arm, was a fixture in his room. My sisters and I took turns, brought magazines from the gift shop, carried coffee that cooled off en route. His feet were cold, so my mother drove home to pick up warmer socks, leaving me to swab his mouth, to listen to his confused concern about getting all the children onto a train. In her short absence, his breath and heartbeat stopped. I was not alone due to the well-timed visit of a familiar chaplain. He reminded me there was no hurry to call the nurse. I was, this time, family, and he had photo ID on a lanyard around his neck. We sat quietly until my mom returned with the socks. The skin on my father's feet? Another 11.5 hours for those padded, shock-absorbing cells to linger. When did my dad leave his body, that bed, the building? I'm convinced it was after my mother re-entered the room.

Pam's daughter Morgan's long-awaited baby is due in May, four months away. The journey is marked with disappointment and despair. When Pam and I talk about this pregnancy, we follow the irrational but time-honoured tradition of knocking on the nearest hard surface; quiet taps, hidden inside pockets and under tables out of sight. We are sitting in her kitchen, perched on stools with Pam's untouched bowl of carrot-ginger soup in front of her. "I talked to Morgan," she says. She sets down her spoon. "Told her I hope I'm here when the baby comes but," the modest side-to-side movement of her head, the shrug of her shoulders are barely visible, "who knows?"

Whoa. It's a long time since we talked about bad outcomes. My current questions have been specific to symptoms or logistics; how was the GO train into the city, and the pain in your left arm, do you have energy for a phone call, want to walk in the woods or the mall? Not once, "How long until you die?" The closest I come is the previous summer when, under the pretence I've found of dropping off a bar of European chocolate, we stand in her front hall. I want to make sure she isn't misconstruing my recent and uncharacteristic displays of level-headedness for lack of care, lack of love. I tell her how devastated I am that this is happening to her, but that I'm trying to match my attitude to hers: positive, practical, composed. If she wants to give a quick medical update and then change the subject, I can do that—can set my distress and anxiety aside so that looking after me isn't an added encumbrance. We hug, and cry. She whispers, "I know, I know."

Pam turns out to be right about the heartbreaking timeline. Date of her death: March 8. Date of Fletcher's birth: May 6. But the question persists. *When does she actually leave?* is now accompanied by *When does the baby actually arrive?* Surely, they exist together in that interval, in a place where it isn't air that sustains life, but love, since her breath has been suspended and his not yet persuaded to begin. I'm tempted, for a moment, to return to the image of clouds, to ease Pam into a wicker rocking chair and place a winged cherub in her arms. But Pam is the best kind of grandmother; one who teaches toddlers to swim, hides coins in birthday cakes, tows a kayak of kids behind her paddleboard. She does not sit still. And so I reposition them; place Fletcher on her chest in a Snugli and send them on forest walks. She kisses his head, names the wildflowers they pass and sets him in her lap at the edge of a lake where she scoops the warm, shallow water over his toes and explains that it's safest to walk out and then swim back. I see her buckle him into a bouncy chair in her kitchen and extend her fingertip to offer a taste of peach jam that, in spite of being runny, is oh so delicious. Two months of post-life, pre-life connection.

Fletcher is born at home; unintended, but not unsafe. When the midwife arrives, she suggests it would be easier to respect the contractions and push than to descend the stairs and climb into the front seat of a car. Not being the one in labour, I can label what comes next as a moment of mystery; breath, blood, exertion, outcry which leaves everyone, especially the newest born, gasping for air.

Annie's bones. My father's skin. And now Pam's tendons? Strands of strong, fibrous tissue that attach muscle to bone. Never having studied anatomy, I tinker with this meaning and when I find another definition that places emphasis on connection, make use of it to solve my dilemma. In life, Pam's ability to connect is well-established; family, friends, neighbours, colleagues all benefit from her kindness and hospitality. If anyone can stretch this out, again with the tendons, to connect the end of one life with the beginning of another, it is Pam.

The midwife leaves and goes home to rest. The next morning, she turns the knob on the unlocked front door and tiptoes to the bedroom in case anyone has been able to sleep. Is this when Pam slips out?

There are valid reasons for shunning Wikipedia as an academic source; the website itself acknowledges that content can be edited by anyone at any moment. Even by me. I return to the page *Clinical Death*; bones, skin, tendons can endure for twelve hours. And I change it to twelve weeks. Should future awareness and discernment cause me to mistrust this calculation, I can always go back and extend it; modify my answer for *When do the dead leave us?* to the more honest *I'm not sure they do*.

X – In (the Shade)

The medicine cabinet in my childhood home was designed to hold, well, medicine. Ours was stocked with aspirin, Band-aids, mercurochrome, Vicks VapoRub; all invaluable to parents with three growing daughters when supplemented with cups of warm, salty water for sore throats, hot lemon and honey for colds, popsicles and ginger-ale for the flu. Milk and bread poultices were prepared for me, the only one susceptible to boils. Gross, I know. One bathroom, one cabinet, and as we got older, new products were added to the shelf. The crocheted rabbit, that crouched on the lid of the tank and hid an extra roll of toilet paper, had to hop over and make room for a basket. Still, the shelves overflowed: Halo shampoo, Johnson's baby oil, Noxzema, Ban cream deodorant, Clearasil, and Muguet des Bois perfume. I expect we kept our elastic sanitary belts and bulky napkins in our bedrooms; an enormous supply when all three of us were old enough to read the "You're a Young Lady Now" booklet. With the exception of Clearasil and toothpaste, the health and beauty products came in glass bottles and jars. We knew to handle them carefully, had not yet been lured by the convenience and safety of plastic, which we've learned is convenient and safe until it overflows in landfills, leaches into our soil, and floats in grotesque pods on the surface of oceans. The bathroom floor, with its multitude of small, black and white hexagonal tiles, would not cushion any accidental fall, but I have no recollection of cleaning up broken glass or removing splinters from the bare heels of my feet. Oh yes, there were tweezers in the cabinet too.

As the youngest of three girls, I took cues from my older sisters; watched and copied what they did in my transition to womanhood. I wish now I'd consulted them before attempting to shave my legs prior to the end-of-school picnic in grade eight. They would have advised me to use shaving cream, or at least lather up the bar of Lifebuoy soap before scraping a razor along my right shin. This released a long curl that resembled decorative icing for a special-occasion cake but was actually skin. They, and that entire generation, did show their own lack of judgement when they slathered themselves with baby oil and set folding lawn chairs in the sun in an attempt to get the perfect tan. Even then, I was suspicious of the heat, the brilliance, the power of the star, which to this day and long before the emoji, I draw as a round yellow ball from which multiple stick arms emanate. I preferred to carry my chair out of the glare and into the shade where the words on the pages of *Seventeen* magazine or a *Nancy Drew* mystery were clear and legible. The sun's westward sweep required me to adjust my chair as the afternoon progressed, inching ever closer to the narrow bed of perennials my mother tended most evenings after dinner while my sisters and I argued over whose turn it was to wash and whose to dry. Peonies, daisies, iris in the sun—lily of the valley in the shade. Had we followed my mother's suggestion and enrolled in the summer program at the children's garden, several blocks away, I would already know the hours of sunlight required by an endless number of plants and not have to look up the subtle distinctions between *direct, indirect,* and *filtered.*

My garden contains lily of the valley too. When we moved to this house nine years ago, Pam noticed, beside the driveway underneath some shrubs, a poorly-lit area that was bare, except for a few weeds that had the potential and network of roots to dominate. "Let me bring you some lily of the valley," she offered. Today when I pick a small handful, rinse out and fill a petite porcelain vase, the fragrance of the tiny blooms nudges my memory, takes me back decades to watch as my oldest sister sprays first her wrists and then her neck with Muguet des Bois cologne. The scent is the same, exactly the same. How did Coty find a chemist in their 1940s lab who was able to match it with such precision? We all know the abysmal failures of the manufacturers of other products like strawberry bubble gum and lemon dishwashing liquid, neither of which smell anything like the original. Curiosity gets the better of me and I consider ordering a bottle to make sure nostalgia isn't making a fool of the olfactory receptors in my nose, but amazon.ca disappoints, yet again. "Currently unavailable." And when I sign into amazon.com, the price is an exorbitant $140 + $45 shipping to drop it at my door. Apparently, it's vintage now. I log out.

Shade intrigues me in both its botanical and figurative forms. It seems I've spent a lifetime holding melancholy's hand, so I'm not sure which of us drags the other from places of activity and enthusiasm onto the sidelines to rest, to observe. Maybe self-identifying as an extrovert, when everyone was dancing to the tune of Myers Briggs, was ill-advised. Shadows, with their connotations of gloom, secrets, and distress, do not appeal to me, but shade does. Horticulturalists, and every adult who had a plot at the children's garden when they were young, know that even "full shade" plants can be exposed to three hours of direct sun each day. Sounds balanced to me. Hidden beneath a canopy of trees, lily of the valley, hostas, forget-me-nots, and I all thrive in low-light conditions.

Now, when restlessness, fatigue, or grief place me in the shade, I remind myself it's a place for contemplation, for renewal, and essential for stepping back and gathering strength to step back in again. I remember that modest light seeps into even the most shaded corners of the garden, if not today then in another season when current obstacles will disperse under a moderated angle of the sun.

XI - Among

There's a grocery store within walking distance of our home. It's not much bigger than the one I walked to as a child, when in exchange for hauling home a glass jug of milk and a paper-wrapped pound of minced beef, I could keep the Lucky Green stamps given to me by the cashier. I licked the stamps, placed them in a booklet provided by the store, and thumbed through the catalogue with its appealing photos and persuasive descriptions of free gifts. Anticipation brought as much pleasure as the objects, though I do recall settling for an umbrella because the coveted ukulele was beyond my reach. My mother redeemed her stamps, a bountiful supply collected on larger, weekly shops, for good juice glasses, not to be confused with the everyday melamine ones buried inside boxes of detergent. Consumers were suckers even then. Dangle stamps, doughnuts, or free shipping in front of us, and we're yours.

There's a superstore within driving distance of our home. It's massive. When it opened, greeters stood by the entrance distributing maps. People who count steps can log several hundred simply because they arrive at the check-out, remember the broccoli, and trek back to the produce section. I head to this store when I need Barry's Tea or flowers that are a step up from the ten-dollar ten-day variety available closer to home. There've been additional trips for Ghirardelli chocolate from the bulk bins, and fig-walnut filone, which when toasted tastes like comfortable feels, but on this particular August day, it's the flowers I'm after.

The selection, like the aisles and carts, is wide and I wander past the modest bunches of single-colour chry-santhemums to stand in front of hefty bouquets, their elegant assortment of blooms slipped into cellophane and secured with raffia belts. It's the peak of local produce in Ontario, but I suspect that most of these stems were grown in Nigeria, then flown to Schiphol Airport. I've seen the Amsterdam flower auction. Bundles spin around a massive warehouse in vehicles that resemble those designed by Fisher-Price, except the Dutch carts have motors and alert drivers with actual limbs instead of wooden torsos that relax into a circular base. The merchandise arrives before midnight and is stored at the appropriate temperature until early morning when traders take their seats in an auditorium and log in. Sales are brisk. Buyers who blink risk going back to their bosses empty-handed. By mid-day all the goods are loaded onto refrigerated trucks or into the chilly cargo holds of planes. Thirty-six hours from field to florist. The planet twists, swirls, and depletes itself to make this happen. Our culture reinforces impatience.

I need two bouquets for an undertaking designed to explore friendship, and have specific requirements in mind. The flowers must vary in type, colour, and size. A few buds are acceptable—greenery too, as long as there is a significant difference in the length and shape of leaves since any distinction by colour is subtle. Everything has to be fresh so I shop on a Tuesday, convinced that the Monday offerings have been rebuffed on the weekend, placed in cold storage, and dragged out again for anyone who forgot an anniversary or is visiting an elderly aunt. Plus, my bouquets have to be identical. It takes a while to meet all of these self-determined criteria and, like every house-hunter in today's real estate market, I have to modify, as in increase, the amount I'm willing to spend. At the check-out, I decline the clerk's offer of gift-wrap sleeves but accept packets of the mysterious chemical that will delay the blossoms' demise. One of these lookalike bouquets comes home with me, the second is given to Tina, my collaborator, and our project, rooted in a conversation about friendship, begins. To be fair...and blunt, the conversation had been about *death* and friendship.

When Pam died my friends, many of whom were also her friends, enfolded me. They dropped off tulips and banana bread and accompanied me on mud-covered trails. They composed emails and sent cards that respected my anguish over the loss of one who for thirty-six years had been my confidante, my crony, my companion in adventure. From the onset of Pam's collision with cancer, Tina would ask, "How's Pam doing?" Then always, "And, how are you?" They had met through me, brought paperbacks and side-dishes to my pot-luck discussions of books. They sat at the same table to celebrate the weddings of my children, and over the years got to know each other as friends of friends do.

Sitting with Tina, weeping about Pam in a sacred space where the tender presence of one did not preclude the painful absence of the other, my heart offered my mind an image. Perhaps "tossed" is more accurate. *Your turn. I need a break.* The image was a bouquet, and it kick-started my brain to examine the particulars of loss in the context of friendship, nudging me from Kleenex to calculations. One spouse, two parents, two siblings, five kids. But friends? A prolific number, with a variety of acquaintances, colleagues, and companions that mirror the diversity in the envisioned bouquet. Logic might say that when X is large, X minus one is no big deal, but logic is no match for a frontal lobe that remembers each in a circle of friends not only by name but by the circumstances of meeting, interests held in common, and the exchange of recipes and ideas. X minus one changes everything.

An Omi and a Bubba, Tina and I spent our lives taking care of our own and educating other people's children and, in retirement, have returned to curiosities that sat on the back burner while spaghetti sauce simmered up front. Our project consists of identical bouquets with daily photographs and commentary to log their changes and inevitable demise, through writing prose (me) and painting an image (her). It is a partnership inspired by an assignment described to me by a fine arts grad on a shared QEW commute. He was paired with an English major who gave him three pieces of her writing. He supplied three pieces of his art in return. His task was to create a visual piece in response to one selection of writing. His partner's? To put in writing a response to the art.

Consider an *ambush of tigers*, a *bloat of hippos*, or a *parliament of owls,* all of which allude to their presence and character while providing us with a collective noun. I'm enticed by *bouquet of friends*, which is more gracious than the term *party of friends* unearthed by Google. This might be appropriate in adolescence but doesn't quite measure up to what we require of each other over the long haul.

Gerbera daisies, sunflowers, a variety of mums, two kinds of lilies (one with no scent which balances the pungency of the other), and a yellow wildflower I recognize but can't name. The greenery, with its ferns, leaves, and branches, enlarges and expands the bouquet so I retrieve and dust off a spacious vase, a wedding gift from my grandmother, and place everything in it. Separating and rearranging stalks, I glimpse four sunflower buds, tight, tiny, as well as three longer, larger buds, and I wonder if they will ever open. Someone slid the gerberas into plastic straws to prevent the weight of the blooms from bending them, breaking them. A few of the carrot-orange petals are wilting. Already.

The mysterious, yellow-budded spikes show up everywhere. I notice them on the trails when walking the dog, beside the path that's a short-cut downtown. It takes a while to identify it as goldenrod, *solidago canadensis*. It would've been faster had the countless photos on Pinterest not been password protected. Social media barters access to their recipes, home décor, and fashion for access to our data and attention. Better to salvage *Reader's Digest Guide to Gardening* from a box in the basement than create another account, or read another cunning introduction to a statement on privacy.

Tina's bouquet is *not* the same as mine. The discrepancies are significant. There's ornamental cabbage in hers but no lilies or goldenrod. Cabbage, how did a vegetable go unnoticed? She is fussy about the greenery and excludes some. I choose not to edit, though I trim the stems and add the packet of white powder that came tucked inside the elastic band. Botanical cocaine.

A flower dies overnight, the gerbera with the droopy petals. I don't detect it until late evening, possibly because its straw case helps it maintain a deceptive, upright posture. "How does it feel when one of the flowers dies?" Tina asks.

If I'm honest, I'm startled that so many are thriving in spite of me watching, waiting, and expecting them to die in this elegant vase that my grief distorts to cracked and half-empty, with a slow leak.

Our endeavour is a lesson in mindfulness, like the one satiated North Americans carry out with a single raisin when asked to observe its folds and their intention to swallow. More lilies open, transforming long, narrow buds into huge blooms, and leaving a third slender one to gather strength for the moment it too will emerge. Maybe the project is really about watching the bouquet take a new shape. Is there room in the-story-I-tell-myself for that?

It's difficult to hold the analogy of friends to flowers lightly. I insert a table into my document and create a one-to-one correspondence that's candid and forthright, matching specific people with the floral inventory taken on day two. Stock-taking: who's the show-stopper, who makes others shine, who hasn't yet peaked, and who is in decline? My attempt is abandoned when I remember that metaphors are compelling because they sidestep our attachment to the intellect and reach into different, deeper places to nudge and elucidate, the right brain gathering up and re-forming the left brain's accumulation of data into an image that holds the essence of meaning while hinting at the details hidden beneath. Besides, the columns look crass.

Our phones recognize the distinction between *contacts* and *favourites,* though Facebook, in its arrogance, labels everyone in its electronic embrace your *friend*. My life includes acquaintances, colleagues, and companions in addition to a handful...no, fistful, of close friends; the ones who sit with me when both my kitchen and inner world are in a state; clutter on the counters plus a jumble of thoughts and emotions piled up and spilling over as if on a rummage-sale table. *Acquaintances* are the people I've met at the leash-free park, or with kids and grand-kids, exploring three different neighbourhoods in this modest-sized town for over forty years. We wave and chat, though I seldom know their last names or what they take in their coffee. In retirement, *colleagues* include the people I used to work with and see on occasion. I also add people I meet through volunteer work and community events. *Companions*, that's harder, but I'll include here the ones who began as acquaintances or colleagues and then migrated to this category after spending more, or more meaning-filled, time together by presenting workshops at conferences, loading bicycles onto cars, or caring for aging parents with comparable declines. The potential remains to develop into *close friend*, though that depends, to some extent, on our locations and available time, but to a greater extent on platonic chemistry. Are the conversations energizing, with flashes of insight? Is there openness to last-minute adventure as well as flexibility to reschedule? Is there some activity each enjoys that is simply more fun when the other tags along? Can you attend their devastation or delight without swerving back to the timeworn, rutted paths of problem-solving or anecdotal comparisons, which intend to show empathy but in fact shove a huge STOP sign in their faces?

In some relationships, I can name the specific moment when a shift occurred. Tina and I had known each other for over a decade when my teen-age daughter waltzed into the kitchen with a piercing that damaged my parental poise more than it did her left eyebrow or her chances of employment. My impulse was to phone Tina. In that era, we were linked by landlines, and since Bell required an additional four dollars a month for caller ID, most of us lifted receivers with no indication of whose voice we would hear. My call was placed mid-cry; messy, desperate crying that prevented sobs and words from being released at the same time. After several minutes, during which Tina comforted me with soft, "Hmm hmms," and gentle "Uh huhs," she quietly asked, "Who is this?" and I knew. She would be good for me.

Today I remove the dead flower. It was pathetic yesterday, especially when taken out of its protective covering, but I tucked it in, propped it up against the others. Stubborn, both of us. I trim all the stems, give the vase a rinse, and fill it with fresh water. Add some sugar to replace the chemical boost currently trickling down the drain. Many of the stems are soft and spongy, and there's wilting that wasn't visible when everything was crowded together in the vase. Mums have a sturdy reputation, but the sunflowers and lilies are the actual stalwarts. The goldenrod looks despondent, but knowing where to source it, I'm tempted to forage—to go at dusk with a pocketknife and cut a few replacement stems. It's not for ethical reasons that I leave nature alone. It's because I've learned, the hard way, that wild flowers prefer, well, the wild. Display them in the dining room and they rebel, go limp, drop tiny insects onto the tablecloth. They might as well be wearing a T-shirt I once saw, and still regret not buying, which said, *Take Me Outside.*

Two gerberas; one is headed for the compost bin, and the other is still its cheeky self, saying, *Look at me. Look how strong, self-sufficient, and beautiful I am*...until I'm not.

A small sunflower opens up. Four buds, but only one unfurls in the uniform conditions of temperature, moisture, and exposure to light. I consider assigning human traits like courage and reticence to explain this; the characteristics of plants, and the index in my gardening book, includes annual/perennial, seed/bulb, but not one reference to personality.

The balance of green and other colours is 60:40, a miniature of the escarpment in early October when coniferous trees, along with their tardy, temperature-sensitive neighbours, provide a solid background for the impressive performance of the crimson, copper, and sienna leaves. This unassuming backdrop is comparable to the one provided by support staff and wives whose steady presence enables others to give the key-note address. Is it the same with friends? Do we slide into familiar roles becoming, yet again, either the humble minion or the histrionic diva? Those patterns were disrupted by my fortieth birthday and the invigorating decision to step away from people who talked non-stop and then asked, "What's new with you?" while rising from the table and reaching into pockets for their keys. These conversations depleted me and I needed to lie down or take an antihistamine for the hives that were forming around my mouth, when I got home.

In the vase, jade and emerald predominate; jewel tones, consistent with the worth of the grid of connections formed by acquaintances and colleagues. I once misunderstood their importance. I selfishly thought of them as understudies to fill gaps or make last-minute substitutions, instead of recognizing them as components in the construction of community. The neighbour who alters their route so a morning walk can be shared and the person who offers encouragement in a spin class are the beams and brackets that scaffold our lives and prevent us from crashing to the ground.

The gerbera never does make it to the green bin. It's been sitting on the bench beside the vessel that holds its fitter, more persistent kin. I find another vase, smaller, unoccupied, and create a second bouquet by moving lifeless stems to this new location. My expectations are low given that the blooms aren't rescued at their peak and hung upside-down in an airy cupboard to dry, which apparently can preserve both colour and shape.

More flowers migrate to the second vase; two stalks of yellow mums and the lily bud that dropped to bob on the surface of the increasingly murky water. A memory of my mother's phone calls surfaces; updates after scouring obituaries, published in either her current or home town paper, accompanied by requests to attend visitations or send a memorial donation at least. Was that her way of telling me she needed a larger vase, somewhere to gather her numerous losses? Tell me that her vase for the dead dwarfed the vase for the living? I was not the only recipient of calls. Others were prompted by entries recorded in an undersized calendar booklet. Deaths, funerals, burials all held significance, but she used a mystifying formula that included length of time since the event, depth of her anguish, and an assumption of the ongoing anguish of others, to determine whether a phone call was warranted. She waited until seven p.m., though she would've preferred the lowest rates that kicked in at eleven. She was a night owl but was aware others were not. Perhaps someone whose number my mother dialed had also been thinking about their lost parent, sibling, or cousin that day, but chances are the person who answered, "Hello" was not. The startling sound of my mother's voice on a random weekday. "Just called to say I'm thinking about you." The receiver, like a hot potato, was tossed to another, who chatted, cautious and confused, anticipating upsetting news, the presumed purpose of the call, which was never delivered. A few days later, the call's recipient would decode the dialogue. It had been six months, or three years, or a decade since a bereavement, an interment, or scattering of ashes across the sea. When my mother died, I became the hesitant heir to this manual and method. My brain synchs with the calendar, and even in retirement stores the date of the next statutory holiday. My husband relies on my prompts for the birthdays of our own children. A comparable, possibly heightened, awareness of time encircles death. Without looking at my phone, I know how many months and days it is since Pam died.

White fluff rests on the bench below the wilting flowers: fragile, light, and soft. It's similar to yet smaller than the tufts on a dandelion, smaller still than the clusters released by milkweed pods when they exhale. I presume it blew in after we slid the door open for the dog until I observe its connection to the gerbera. Winged seeds have developed at the base of each petal, an extravagant number confirming nature's no-nonsense response to the multitude of hazards on regeneration's road. Seeds, germination, blooms, seeds. I've never kept flowers long enough to see more than a sliver of this progression, but now I'm waiting to see what comes after what was supposed to be the end.

The surviving sunflower, Peruvian lilies, button mums, and ferns are trimmed and take up residence in a third, smaller vase, which refreshes them and causes me to look at them with new eyes. When I let them be what they are and for the moment set aside what's missing, I stop noticing the gaps and realize I have a handsome bouquet. It's unlike the one I started with, but still. A creature, probably a mouse, has helped itself to pieces of the sunflower. I heard something scurrying between the floorboards. The invitation to come inside was intended only for particular delegates from the natural environment that lies beyond my screened porch, but apparently rodents can't read.

The contents of all three vases are emptied into the green bin today. I anticipate a profound, mystical experience. Instead, my brain struggles to recall if plants are listed in the pamphlet that outlines acceptable items for inclusion and pick up. The profound experience comes later in the day. It shouts *Gotcha* when I write to Tina about my driveway expedition and Gmail, knowing my habits but without asking permission, adds Pam's name to the list of recipients. This is where artificial intelligence reveals its heartless limitations...by suggesting I can click on her underlined name and bring her back to place Post-it notes on the Rand McNally road maps, set her Friday dinner table with crystal, and express intolerance for unmade beds.

No longer limited to twenty-four exposures or required to wait days for processing, Tina and I have an abundance of photos, available immediately. We each select our favourites and are scrolling through the shared folder when Tina asks, "Which flower do you think represents Pam?" In spite of my previous rationale for not establishing a one-to-one correspondence, I've been watching the bouquet with precisely that question in mind. *Which flower represents Pam?* The gerbera is a reasonable choice, since to be truthful, it is the first flower to die. It is also tall, bright, and confident until you notice the opaque straw that props it up, though that too could be interpreted as the radiation and chemo she received to keep *her* upright, all of which would make the gerbera a contender. Another candidate is the goldenrod, the wildflower assigned to only my bouquet. I'm now in the habit of looking for it. I know it grows next to the rigorous trails we hiked weekly for decades until her decline required an alternate route, compelling us to swallow our pride and walk meekly, weakly in the mall. Like Pam, the goldenrod flourishes outside. My relentless quest to track it down keeps me *forest bathing* on days when I'm inclined to nap, providing me with an opportunity to relax, to stretch, to breathe, much like other events she hosted. I take pictures of it in every season and plan witty comments to accompany them on-line but the flowers are hazy, elusive. The foreground tussles with the background, and in spite of the edit options on Instagram, I press cancel.

Tina chooses an early photo of the bouquet. Its composition appeals to her. The modest decline of a few petals adds interest—hints at what's to come. I presume she unwraps a blank canvas right away until I ask her. She describes beginning with a thumbnail sketch on a piece of paper that's the same size as the canvas she's chosen. The photograph on her iPad, unlike the bouquet in its vase, is static, permitting as many minutes as she needs to discern and draw the shapes. No consideration of colours yet. Only shapes. Then she dips her brush in a pale shade and paints the same thumbnail on canvas; somewhat similar to writing a first draft, except I can tap Ctrl A Delete and no one's the wiser. Paint has more endurance, causing me to wonder if revisions remain noticeable under subsequent, more confident strokes; faint, barely visible reminders of missteps like the ones we made writing term papers and attempted to conceal under Wite-Out decades ago. The small bottles we kept on desks and in pencil cases are redundant today, mistaken by contemporary students for nail polish.

The room where Tina paints has a north-facing window. Clear, soft light slides into the room, a generous amount despite the position of its source. The area expanded when she collapsed the folding table that always used to be covered with daunting piles of report cards and at least one mug of lukewarm tea. It's the only room in the house that is hers alone, cunningly devoid of board games, electronics, and snacks that could entice both family and guests. There's an easel, a selection of brushes, numerous tubes of paint, and her recently acquired guide to mixing colours, an intervention to prevent the production of muddy, sludge-like shades, reminiscent of kindergarten playdough on a Friday afternoon. My assumption had been she would glance at her chosen subject and without delay squeeze a daub of this, a dab of that to blend the desired hue; a hypocritical notion since Microsoft has already intervened on behalf of writers, providing a thesaurus, spellcheck, and a grammarian which prompts *Instead of, Consider* to keep us on track.

There's a ritual to setting up her room and steps Tina follows each time she paints. Two jars and an egg carton are rescued from the bag of recycling. The former are filled with water, the latter provides a place to set brushes; higher callings than the one awaiting shampoo bottles and newsprint, which loiter by the back door until someone escorts them to the curb. She returns to the kitchen to make a hot drink. While the kettle boils, she places nine chocolate-covered almonds in a dish. This precision catches me by surprise, but perhaps ritual is more about preparing *her* to paint than it is about preparing the room. Like the tennis player who bounces the ball a specific number of times before each serve, or the concert pianist who adjusts the bench a little to the left, a little to the right, before landing fingers on the first chord, Tina has a routine that marks the beginning of this time set apart from accustomed roles and tasks. She'll be embarrassed when I identify this as a transition from woman to artist, but that's what it is.

After an hour and a half, sometimes less, Tina descends to the basement, lathers up a bar of soap, and washes her brushes in the laundry-room sink. She stops for the day at either extreme of the continuum between stuck and satisfied. The unfinished painting is set on a ledge in the dining room. She looks at it often. If she is stuck at the end of a session, she scrutinizes the painting to discern a way forward. If she is satisfied, she plans her next step, which will make it easier to get started next time—make it easier, in fact, to enter the room. Scrutiny, planning, but no basking in either her accomplishment or ability. Girls in the '50s were taught that was bold. We were given embroidery thread and patterns to iron onto tea towels, one for each day. We stitched kittens who grinned through their washing, ironing, mending, shopping, cleaning, and baking, and then rested on Sundays, unless you consider preparing a hot meal for your entire extended family to be work. The kittens hid their paintbrushes and books along with their talent.

An artist friend studies the painting and suggests Tina add blue, in spite of there being no evidence of it in the actual bouquet or its photographic representation. She adds blue, then catches her breath as the previously painted blooms come to life, stand a little taller, and stop leaning on each other. The blue paint? I don't even notice it until she describes the technique to me. Her explanation includes the word *value* in an unfamiliar way; not signifying worth but as it's used by artists. It shouldn't surprise me that this profession has a unique lexicon—every profession does. When studying engineering, my husband and his peers joked about *necking in bars,* which for those who wear an iron ring, refers to the narrowing of a piece of metal when it is stretched. In this age of sexting and Tinder, the play on words is tame, archaic. Tina explains that the *value* of a colour is a measure of its lightness and darkness in contrast to the *hue,* which is the colour itself, and the *intensity*, which is the level of saturation. I nod as if I understand.

The blue intrigues me. I find an image of the colour wheel and locate blue opposite orange and yellow, an exact match to the gerberas and sunflowers that dominate the bouquet. Blue is their complement, which means when placed next to each other they wake each other up, make each other shine. Aha! I'm on a roll, and since the internet's been turned back on, I continue to pursue blue and come across a long list related to its symbolism in art. Much of it is abstract and idealistic: tranquility, stability, unity. Others, like sky, water, or depression, are predictable. But appetite suppressant? That makes no sense at all.

Then it hits me. Since Pam died five months before our project began, maybe she's not represented by a flower after all. Maybe she's best epitomized by the blue paint, which can be present, unnoticed or detected but clarifies everything else. Friendship, loss, gratitude, death. She pulls me into all of it. Is this too big a leap? I revisit the notes made after talking with Tina about the role of blue in art and discover I highlighted *trust, truth* when I cut and pasted the symbol list. This increases my confidence. It's as if Pam, a task-person, a teacher, and the first close friend to die, has given me homework; a variation on the word problems that separate the number-loving sheep from the number-loathing goats in elementary school. If two friends are travelling at the same speed on trains headed to the same destination, but one gets derailed, how does the other one get to the station? Figure this out and subsequent losses, like pop quizzes and mid-terms, can be endured, and the final exam of my own death will not cast a terrifying shadow over every source of light. This is the value of blue.

The groceries I carry home today are unwieldy. Gravity and cans of diced tomatoes tug the shopping bags toward the sidewalk, wrenching my arms to the scraping rhythm of cloth meeting pavement. When the bags are hoisted up, slung over each shoulder, their weight settles in a different place, and the route home, in spite of its incline, is manageable. Maybe loss can be carried this way too. Perhaps in addition to the better-known centre of gravity, around which we balance and distribute mass, there's also a centre of grief for the balance and distribution of misery. All the heavy stuff.

Dinner guests often bring wine, frequent visitors a salad, but tonight Tina arrives with the painting, her gift to me. It's exquisite. The radio and its hosts on CBC are demoted to the bottom shelf of the small table beside my desk to clear space for it. My eyes drift from the keyboard to the canvas, which sits close enough to identify the miniscule font of her signature, the raised curls of acrylic, and the radiant abundance of blue. Most days this brings great joy, but it's also a reminder that the bouquet of friends I have now is a different one. It has been transformed.

XII - Within

Two weeks after the death of my father, 1 flew to the southern hemisphere. My husband had a five-month research opportunity in New Zealand, so 1 took a leave of absence from teaching and prepared our school-age children for a semester where vowels were flipped and uniforms worn. Drained by the flight and wading through grief, 1 appreciated the advice and tips offered by neighbours and other sojourners but struggled to absorb them. "Don't use the sun to get your bearings," cautioned a Canadian who'd emigrated a decade earlier. "Its place in the sky will throw you off." Huh? Do people do that? Look at the sky to figure out where they are? Lots of people, apparently, and while the sun continues to rise in the east and set in the west, its path arches across the northern sky in the southern hemisphere, the opposite of its familiar arc in Canada where it sweeps across the south. Evidently vowels are not the only items that flip.

The sky can impact people within Canada too. Consider a woman from Gimli, Manitoba, who floundered in discussions that took place after she moved to Southern Ontario where we met. She claimed that growing up under a vast sky far from neighbours contributed not only to her independence and self-sufficiency but also to her strongly-held, boldly-proclaimed opinions. There was capacity for an abundance of words under that sky. When there were clashes in community conversations, everyone retreated, reconsidered, and renewed efforts the next time they met, which in all likelihood and to some advantage, was not for several weeks. In our congested, built-up Golden Horseshoe, it's impossible to look twenty feet ahead without a vehicle, structure, or person coming into view. Haze and high-rises occupy most of our sky, leaving a mere sliver for the audacious few who long to look up. In this context, people interrupt, interject, talk over and around but hardly ever *to* each other. When we disagree with companions or colleagues, we are squeezed back into close proximity the next time we use an elevator, or check out 1-8 items in the grocery store. It's doubtful that the term passive-aggressive was coined on an acreage. An increase in elbow room results in a decrease in jabs, an inverse ratio that caged rats have always understood.

No, the sun and the sky weren't the primary influence when I was growing up in Hamilton or residing as an adult in neighbouring Dundas. It was, and still is, the Niagara Escarpment, shortened by locals to escarpment since

Niagara implies the falls, the border, and more recently, wine. This ridge of dolomite splits the city into below and on *the mountain*. Immigrants and visitors who've seen the Andes and Himalayas are confused that a hundred-metre change in elevation warrants this designation. Long-term residents use it as a point of reference, especially in the lower city. We pivot, scan, locate the escarpment, whisper "south," and find our way. We don't need Google maps or a passerby's rambling instructions, which invariably include "across from Tim's" at least once. Newcomers from Toronto are thankful for this option since the location of Lake Ontario muddles them. When they'd packed their bags and given notice on their unaffordable flats, the lake had been to their south. Now on James Street at an *Art Crawl*, they're startled to see the lake has drifted north, but are reassured, to some extent, when they catch a glimpse of the mountain and find it has stayed put.

For six decades I've lived minutes from jagged cliffs, hustling streams, and an assortment of waterfalls. From my desk in an east-facing bay window, I lean forward and look left. There between our rust-coloured bricks and a recently-installed traffic light lies a wedge of the escarpment, less than two kilometres away. In the opposite direction, the escarpment sits five hundred metres farther, my view of it obscured until the trees on my neighbour's lawn give in to winter, lay down their leaves, and scatter walnuts to the restless squirrels below. Even when I can't see it, I know it's there, solid, unchanging, like a theatre backdrop in front of which scenery is positioned and the action occurs. The configuration of the Dundas Valley includes a third, less conspicuous section behind me, to the west. Historic Governors Road climbs up this ramp of glacial debris, its undulations unnoticed by drivers who power up and over them. Cyclists, who have to adjust gears and speed, lose patience when it takes eight kilometres to reach the highpoint. They opt instead for Weir's Lane or Sydenham Hill. Intense, short-lived exertion.

So, if the expansive prairie sky hovering over a sparse population afforded my friend self-assurance and candour, what was the upshot of dwelling in this place where ancient ice crept one step forward, two steps back, where limestone and magnesium joined forces to create a tougher, more resistant caprock, which much like fondant over a multi-layered cake, protects what lies beneath? When I hiked fifty-three times on the Bruce Trail, that 900-kilometre ribbon of wilderness that weaves among cliffs, streams, and waterfalls, and returned each time to my home in the arc of this U-shaped valley, I realized that the escarpment has been a formative, transcendent presence in my life, which were an analogy required, felt like an arm around my shoulder. Initially, the recognition of this image and sensation was a relief. As an anxious earthling, the idea that the terrain of the planet itself could shelter and comfort appealed to me. But then, I panicked. What if living here had created my anxiety? What if my unconscious self was so accustomed to dwelling within this robust ridge that I faltered beyond it? Theories about volatility in the valley churned until the long-standing image of "Which came first?" emerged. Had the proverbial egg turned me into a chicken?

Maybe I had clucked, flapped, and wobbled through prior phases, but a lot has happened in the eight years since Pam and I began our Bruce Trail adventure, even more in the four years since we completed it end-to-end; my gracious, sensible mother declined and died; massive allergy-test welts on my back were photographed as exemplars of extreme; a rambunctious puppy was welcomed and returned; and a kind but candid social worker offered insights, strategies, and a context in which to connect some dots. I retired from teaching and Pam, lovely and much-loved, died. I'm taking another look at the escarpment and the trail and their significance in my less anxious and somewhat grounded life.

What exactly happened to me while putting one foot in front of the other, repeating that action a million times to reach Tobermory? What happened while we were *forest bathing?* The phrase evokes swimsuits but is, in fact, a translation from Japanese, *Shinrin-yoku,* which describes the profound, positive effect that spending time in nature has on mood, energy, and well-being. My conclusion can be distilled to my experience of this trifecta: the air, the earth, and an ally.

Forests have a canopy but no roof, making the sky the limit for copious amounts of clean air. Add to that the ingenious design and performance of trees by which they not only provide us with oxygen but also mop up our carbon dioxide. Some of it, and for the time being. On the trail we could taste the sweet, weightless air. After gruelling ascents, gulps replaced inhalations. After nimble descents, we rubbed our knees, panting modest mouthfuls 'til the pain subsided. The air remained sweet, weightless. It floated into my lungs and crossed borders, plumping up cells to sail their cargo of energy to the rest of the body. Oh, the O_2. I appreciated anew the airlines' directive to don and activate my own emergency mask before assisting others. How many times had I tugged on a plastic cup and adjusted the elastic band in someone else's life? Now I reserved non-teaching days for hiking and B&Bs that offered shuttling, aligning myself with mystics and musicians for whom deep breaths and complete exhalations are mandatory.

Our hiking boots landed on moss, water, stone, mud, rock. Regardless of the surface, it seemed each step put pressure on a power button hidden beneath, prompting the earth to release energy from its ancient, abundant store. Topographical endorphins. Could they have travelled not only through layers of clothing to locate and strengthen muscles, but also through layers of resistance to locate and strengthen my sense of self? I was becoming realistic, practical, down-to-earth because of the earth.

Finally, an ally. It was not difficult for acquaintances back home, or observant hikers and hosts we met on the trail, to discover the similarities Pam and I shared; athletic educators, long-married mothers, dog-walking grandmas, outgoing bakers, responsible volunteers. Sketch a Venn diagram and the mutual attributes would enlarge the overlapping circles until only slim crescents of divergence remained, but that divergence was formidable and impacted the way we walked on the earth before we walked together on the trail. Me? A hand-wringer. Pam?

She pulled up her socks. For 900 kilometres we had front-row seats in each other's lives, witnessing reactions and responses to a range of events and circumstances as they unfolded, creatures of our respective habits until we heard accounts of familiar dilemmas with more favourable outcomes. My long-standing pattern of hesitate-act-regret-ponder-repeat was not working for me. Me and my socks were in a slump, which made me keen, if not desperate, for alternatives. From Pam 1 learned that multi-angled speculation and analysis are exhausting as well as unproductive, and that when nervous energy is properly channelled, both impenetrable anxiety and overgrown shrubs get pruned back. Perhaps from watching me, Pam learned to linger, to value good enough as an option. 1 never asked.

That notion of a geophysical arm around my shoulder? I'm shaking it off, trading it in for an image of a hand resting lightly on my back, between and just below my shoulders; a reminder, to some extent, of the escarpment's tough, resistant caprock, and reassurance that 1 can access its energy again and again. *Shinrin-yoku.* Air, earth—breathing, walking—strength and resilience replenished. To a greater extent, the handprint is a tender reminder of either Pam's ongoing presence in my life or her significant legacy. It depends on which side of my brain is calling the shots on any given day, steering me toward the mystical or the material world.

Because 1 live where 1 live, the escarpment is in my peripheral vision on every errand and outing. It's there when 1 saunter downtown with my refillable coffee cup. It's there when 1 hop on my bike, coast into the city, and grind back home. It's there outside the GO train window, its distance both south and north of the tracks increasing as it accommodates Lake Ontario, leaving space for the suburbs to sprawl. It's the last natural feature I observe when driving to the airport, and spotting it from a descending plane is the best part of my flight home. Having hiked its length and knowing that the Bruce Trail weaves on, beside, and below the escarpment, I gaze at whatever section is in sight, wiping smudged bifocals in an attempt to see past the trees, through the undergrowth, to locate the fragile ribbon of our route. When possible, I pin detailed memories as well as vague sensations onto it. A chilly hilltop picnic, a misinterpreted map, an ill-fitting boot, a mud-splattering skid, a burgundy trillium; contentment, hilarity, fatigue, panic, and delight merging to create an unanticipated avenue of breadcrumbs; points of light that flicker dimly, glow steadily, and shine ferociously like the fickle strands of illumination we hang in December but crave all year round.

Afterword

Friendship, Loss, and the Bruce Trail; some may pick up this volume based on an interest in all three, but it's more likely that one aspect of this subtitle holds more appeal. Some may also enjoy taking apart the strands that bring these components together, but for the less patient, for those who haven't built up detangling skills when balancing a curly-haired toddler on their lap, I've separated out what I've come to know about each of the three facets. If you wish you'd known about this section sooner, I apologize. It wasn't possible for me to distill it this way until I had 20,000 other words written down. The good news is that the trail itself, if you are attentive and inclined to hiking, is delineated with less ambiguity, and will not disappoint you in the same way.

Friendship

▶Connect with people of different ages, stages, and backgrounds. ▶Balance in-person visits, where you breathe the same air, with e-visits; emojis are over-worked and over-rated. ▶Initiate conversations with people who are alone at parties, in lecture halls, at reunions. You'll have someone to talk to, and they will be grateful. ▶Avoid gossip. "I'm not supposed to tell you this but..." is an enormous red flag. ▶Value companionship. Who you are walking with is as important as the direction you're heading. ▶Keep the bar for entertaining low. Tables can be set without charger plates. Saying "I made it myself," takes several seconds, which is hours less than the time required to make anything from scratch. ▶Listen. Two ears, one mouth. ▶Remember details, or if that's a challenge, write them down. When you're next together, ask about the premature niece, or the night-school course. ▶Don't keep track of hosting. Taking turns is not always feasible, but do remember who you owe for tickets. ▶Explain a change or cancellation with "I'm running out of steam." This gives others permission to measure their own energy and strive for balance. ▶Don't easily take offence. Not everyone can be invited to weddings. ▶Some life events put friendship on the backburner; care of elderly parents, the arrival of babies and grandbabies. ▶Give specific options of help. "Can I bring chili, or lasagna?" is better than, "Let me know if there's anything I can do." ▶Show up. ▶Tell close friends you love them. Use other phrases to express appreciation and affection for acquaintances, colleagues, and companions, or borrow this; "The day/walk/work/work-out goes better when you are here!" ▶Step away from the people who leave you exhausted or demoralized. ▶Don't expect all of your friends to get along. ▶Invite your partner to meet your friends and their partners. If it's fun, repeat; if it's not, lesson learned. ▶Send snail-mail cards, drop off flowers that are already in a vase. ▶Ask, "Is this a good time?" when you call. ▶Shun phrases like, "We'll have to get together sometime." Calendar apps are poised to add events and even send notifications to remind you. ▶Spend time with people who share and embolden your curiosities. ▶If you are an introvert, shy, or short on conversation skills, ask people the questions they've just asked you. ▶Booths are better than tables. ▶Forward a modest number of photos and even fewer jokes, but absolutely no variations on the chain letter. ▶Enjoy your friendships but don't expect everything to stay the same; sparkle tarnishes, despair also lifts.

Loss

▶Concede that death is the original disruptor, older by millennia than the innovators and entrepreneurs who toss the term around today. ▶Say, "Hello grief" on days when you feel restless, agitated, sad. ▶Go outside. ▶Spend time with children, grandchildren, dogs. ▶Tell people you are grieving. Unless you own a black veil or a T-shirt with *This is the worst day ever*, printed on it, how are they to know? ▶Be mindful of the many forms grief takes. Don't expect to grieve the same way that others do, or even the same way you did after previous losses. ▶ Create a loss playlist, or borrow mine: *Adagio for Strings*, Samuel Barber; *In the Valley*, Jane Siberry sung by K.D. Lang; *For Good*, Stephen Schwartz sung by Kristen Chenoweth and Idina Menzel; *This Bitter Earth*, Clyde Otis sung by Dinah Washington. ▶ Cry. If you need to prime the pump, the playlist will be of assistance. The soundwaves of instruments, especially strings, resonate tenderly through cracks and despair. ▶ Think about how you handle stress; loss is a kind of stress. Embrace strategies that support rest and healing, and avoid the self-destructive ones— *Sauvignon blanc,* step back. ▶ Bear in mind that loss does not begin when breathing ends. It begins when the qualities and abilities you love in a person wither or decline, when the knitter can't follow patterns, when the scholar holds books upside down, when the baseball fan loses track of innings. ▶ Pay attention. ▶ Take complete turns when talking about loss with others. Don't alternate in snippets. Listen fully to their story before telling yours. If some can't do this, find others who can. ▶ Walk, cycle, run. ▶ Put the WeCroak app on your phone. They've sifted through quotes about death, then offer the wisest ones so users can contemplate mortality five times a day. The arrival of notifications is random. Remind you of anything? ▶ Create a loss compartment. Tuck your lost beloved inside to fortify you, and eventually to welcome and carry others who follow. ▶ Forest bathe, *shinrin-yoku*, without headphones. ▶ Beware the change of seasons. Loss may recharge itself as light diminishes or temperatures rise. ▶ Respect all losses, but there's a hierarchy. Pet owners who've euthanized an elderly dog do *not* know what it's like to deliver a stillborn child. ▸ Expect the emotions connected to past losses to resurface with current or future ones. This is why some of us weep at the funerals of people we don't know well, such as distant cousins and the parents of colleagues. ▸ Resist the allure of ease and distraction. Unattended pain comes back. Always.

Bruce Trail

▸ Join the Bruce Trail Conservancy and buy their reference guide. ▸ Put their app on your phone if it will support, but not distract you. ▸ Check that all hikers are using the same edition of maps. Learn to read the contours. ▸ Break in new boots; a little too big is better than a little too small. The opposite is true for daily distance; too short is better than too long. ▸ Ignore the blue side trails unless needed to access the main trail. ▸ Make lunches that include protein but aren't temperature sensitive. ▸ Buy sunscreen and insect repellent in separate tubes. The combination is tempting but less effective. ▸ Take two sets of car keys. ▸ Put your water bottle in the side pocket of another person's backpack. ▸ Be creative with both the order and direction of the hikes; tap into your knowledge of antonyms to translate route descriptions intended for south to north travel. ▸ Take along the map you need plus the one that follows. ▸ Study options for lengthening or shortening a route should circumstances require it. ▸ Phone each other after rising on mornings with a pre-dawn start. Everyone will sleep better. ▸ Capitalize on trips that require accommodation by arriving at the B&B in the morning and hiking a full day before staying overnight.▶When packing for multi-day excursions, consider what you will wear on the hottest day, the coldest day, the wettest day. No bad weather, just bad clothing.▶Use motels, buses, and taxis in urban areas.▶Split all costs. If one drives, the other pays for gas.▶Keep old towels and extra running shoes in the trunk.▶Always shuttle in the morning, never in the afternoon. Park your car at the end point of the hike. Shuttle (recruit friends or B&B hosts) to the start of the hike.▶Use the plastic map-sleeve that comes in the guide book and wear it on a lanyard around your neck. Put a whistle on the lanyard.▶Dress in layers, socks too. Figure out which items are comfortable and wear them again and again.▶Hike the road sections on rainy days.▶Enjoy hot beverages before or after, but not during the hike. Tea and coffee always taste like the thermos, worse if you add dairy.▶Hike with people who walk at your speed. Set your own goals unless you are attempting to beat the FKT nine days.▶Use poles.▶Stop for water.▶Figure out a comfortable position for nature pees. If aging knees prevent squatting, hold onto a small tree and lean back, or perch on the edge of a fallen log.▶Keep snacks in pockets to eat on-the-go but sit and rest with lunch.▶Check opening hours for stores and cafes in the off-season or in rural areas. 24/7 is a Southern Ontario thing.▶Avoid deadlines or evening commitments on hiking days.▶Redeem mistakes, missteps, and miscalculations with the phrase *in the spirit of the trail.*▶Put one foot in front of the other. Repeat.

Acknowledgements

Warm thanks and great affection are extended to the
following people (and one dog):
Al Will, Megan Medlock, Morgan Will, and Patti Smith
for letting me tell the stories,
Tina Van Beveren for endless wisdom and for painting
the flower project,
Sue Graham, Judy Michel, and Judy Pollard Smith for
reading and responding (quickly!) to every draft,
Eva Jackson for taking the photo at Queenston
Heights Park

Family and friends in my current bouquet, and the ones,
like Pam,
now resting elsewhere, for inspiration
and encouragement

In the Shade

The Bruce Trail Conservancy for their reference guide, maps and app, their past motto *Close to Nature, Close to Home*, and their current *Preserving a Ribbon of Wilderness, for Everyone, Forever*

The team and editors at FriesenPress for assistance in improving and publishing this collection

Art for being in my corner, always, and Blossom for napping under my desk

Printed in Canada